MAYER SMITH

The Eternal Caravan

Copyright © 2025 by Mayer Smith

All rights reserved. No part of this publication may be reproduced, stored or transmitted in any form or by any means, electronic, mechanical, photocopying, recording, scanning, or otherwise without written permission from the publisher. It is illegal to copy this book, post it to a website, or distribute it by any other means without permission.

This novel is entirely a work of fiction. The names, characters and incidents portrayed in it are the work of the author's imagination. Any resemblance to actual persons, living or dead, events or localities is entirely coincidental.

Mayer Smith asserts the moral right to be identified as the author of this work.

Mayer Smith has no responsibility for the persistence or accuracy of URLs for external or third-party Internet Websites referred to in this publication and does not guarantee that any content on such Websites is, or will remain, accurate or appropriate.

Designations used by companies to distinguish their products are often claimed as trademarks. All brand names and product names used in this book and on its cover are trade names, service marks, trademarks and registered trademarks of their respective owners. The publishers and the book are not associated with any product or vendor mentioned in this book. None of the companies referenced within the book have endorsed the book.

First edition

*This book was professionally typeset on Reedsy.
Find out more at reedsy.com*

Contents

1	A Chance Encounter	1
2	The Song of the Caravan	8
3	Whispers in the Wind	15
4	The Vanishing Map	22
5	A Thread Between Us	29
6	The Woman in the Cloak	35
7	Threads of Yesterday	42
8	The Forbidden Dance	49
9	The First Betrayal	56
10	The Marked Book	62
11	The Caravan's Curse	68
12	A Pact with the Shadows	76
13	The Mirror of Truth	83
14	The Caravan Attacked	90
15	The Stolen Map	97
16	The Maze of Shadows	104
17	A Heart Divided	111
18	The Caravan Fractures	118
19	The Eternal Sacrifice	124
20	The Last Dance	131
21	Love Beyond Time	138
22	The Eternal Caravan Restored	144

One

A Chance Encounter

The rain had been relentless for hours, a curtain of silver needles lashing the earth with a ferocity that seemed almost personal. Liora pulled her shawl tighter around her shoulders, though it did little to shield her from the cold. The sky above was an endless gray, darkened further by the encroaching night. The dirt road beneath her boots had turned to mud, sucking at her feet with each step as she trudged forward, the weight of her small satchel growing heavier with every passing moment.

Her destination was a village she had never seen, a name she had overheard in passing at the last tavern where she had found shelter. But that had been days ago, and now the isolation pressed in on her like the walls of a cage. The road stretched endlessly ahead, and though she knew she should have stopped to rest hours earlier, the growing unease at the storm's intensity drove her forward.

The first sign of the Caravan came as a low hum, a haunting melody carried on the wind, just barely audible over the drumming rain. Liora froze mid-step, her breath catching in her throat. She scanned her surroundings, her heart quickening. There was no one else on the road, no lights in the distance, no sound of approaching horses or wagons—only the song. It was beautiful, but it set her teeth on edge, as though the tune itself carried an unspoken warning.

"Hello?" she called out, her voice hoarse from disuse. It was swallowed instantly by the storm.

The song faded as suddenly as it had come, leaving only the sound of the rain. Liora shivered, glancing over her shoulder. Nothing but the empty road and the dark outline of the forest beyond. She shook her head, forcing herself to move forward again. It was just her imagination. The storm was playing tricks on her mind.

Then she saw him.

He appeared on the road as though conjured from the mist, a solitary figure standing motionless in the rain. His dark cloak billowed around him, the hood drawn low to obscure his face. He stood with an unnatural stillness, his head tilted as though listening to something she could not hear. Liora's heart leapt into her throat. Every instinct screamed at her to turn and run, but her feet refused to obey. She clutched her satchel tighter, her knuckles whitening.

A Chance Encounter

"Who's there?" she demanded, her voice trembling but firm.

The man didn't respond. Instead, he lifted his head slightly, just enough for her to glimpse the sharp line of his jaw and the pale glint of his eyes beneath the hood. His gaze locked onto hers, and Liora felt a strange pull in her chest, as though an invisible thread had just tightened between them.

"You shouldn't be out here alone," the man said finally, his voice low and smooth, like the first rumble of thunder before a storm.

"I could say the same to you," Liora retorted, though her voice lacked the confidence she intended. "Who are you?"

He stepped closer, the mud beneath his boots squelching with each deliberate stride. Liora instinctively backed away, her pulse racing. Her hand went to the small knife hidden in her satchel, though she doubted she'd have the courage to use it if it came to that.

"I mean you no harm," he said, stopping a few paces away. He pushed back his hood, revealing a face that was both rugged and elegant, with sharp cheekbones and piercing gray eyes that seemed to hold secrets far older than he could be. His dark hair clung to his forehead, drenched from the rain.

Liora hesitated. There was something disarming about him, something that made her feel as though he belonged here in a way she never could. Yet the unease remained, coiling tighter around her chest.

"I didn't ask if you meant harm," she said, trying to sound braver than she felt. "I asked who you are."

The man's lips quirked in a faint smile, though it didn't reach his eyes. "Eryx," he said simply. "And you?"

"Liora," she said before she could stop herself. She cursed inwardly at her own foolishness. A stranger on a deserted road, and she was already giving him her name?

Eryx's gaze lingered on her for a moment, as though he were committing her face to memory. "Liora," he repeated, the name rolling off his tongue with an odd familiarity. "You're not from here."

It wasn't a question, but she answered anyway. "No. Just passing through."

"In this storm?" His tone was skeptical, but there was something else in it, a curiosity she couldn't place. "Where are you headed?"

"To the next village," she said, lifting her chin defiantly. "Why? Are you planning to follow me?"

His smile widened slightly, and for a moment, she thought she saw a flicker of amusement in his eyes. "You wound me, Liora. I'm not the one you should fear out here."

"Then who should I fear?" she challenged, though her voice trembled slightly. The rain was beginning to soak through her shawl, chilling her to the bone.

Eryx didn't answer right away. He glanced over his shoulder, toward the forest, as though expecting someone—or something—to emerge from the shadows. When he looked back at her, his expression was serious. "The road ahead isn't safe. The storm isn't natural."

Liora frowned. "What are you talking about? It's just a storm."

"It's never just a storm," he said quietly. There was a weight to his words, a certainty that made her stomach tighten.

Before she could respond, the haunting melody returned, louder this time, weaving through the rain like a phantom's whisper. Liora's breath hitched as she turned her head toward the sound. It seemed to come from everywhere and nowhere at once.

"What is that?" she asked, her voice barely audible over the song.

Eryx didn't answer. Instead, he grabbed her wrist and pulled her off the road, toward the shelter of a large oak tree. His grip was firm but not painful, and she was too startled to resist.

"Stay quiet," he murmured, his eyes scanning the road.

Liora opened her mouth to protest, but the words died in her throat when she saw them. Figures began to emerge from the mist, their forms indistinct at first, like shadows given shape.

The Eternal Caravan

They moved in eerie unison, their faces obscured by hoods, their movements almost hypnotic. The melody grew louder as they drew closer, a haunting symphony that made her skin crawl.

Eryx's grip on her wrist tightened. "Don't move," he whispered.

The figures passed by without stopping, their cloaks billowing around them like specters. Liora's heart pounded in her chest, her breath coming in shallow gasps. She dared not move, dared not even blink until the last of them had disappeared into the storm.

When the road was empty once more, Eryx released her wrist and stepped back. "Now do you understand?" he asked softly.

Liora stared at him, her mind racing with questions she couldn't begin to articulate. "What were they?" she finally managed.

"Not something you want to meet," he said grimly. "You're lucky I found you first."

"Lucky?" she repeated, her voice rising with a mix of fear and anger. "I don't feel very lucky right now."

Eryx met her gaze, his expression unreadable. "You should. The Eternal Caravan isn't known for mercy."

Liora's blood ran cold. "The Eternal Caravan?" she echoed. "What is that?"

A Chance Encounter

Eryx's eyes darkened, and for the first time, she saw a flicker of something akin to fear in his gaze. "A curse," he said simply. "And now that they've seen you, you're part of it."

Two

The Song of the Caravan

The night seemed darker after the strange figures disappeared into the storm. Liora stood frozen under the ancient oak, the cold rain dripping from its gnarled branches. Her heart was still pounding in her chest, the eerie melody lingering in her ears. Eryx stood a few feet away, his cloak plastered to his lean frame, his gray eyes watching her closely, as though waiting for her to collapse under the weight of the fear she had no words to express.

"You said they've seen me," Liora said, her voice trembling. "What does that mean?"

Eryx didn't answer immediately. Instead, he turned his gaze toward the road where the spectral figures had vanished. The wind carried with it faint echoes of the melody, as if mocking her question. When he finally spoke, his voice was low, as if he feared the storm might overhear.

"The Eternal Caravan doesn't pass unnoticed," he said. "Once they see you, they leave a mark. It's not something you can escape."

Liora felt a chill that had nothing to do with the rain. "A mark? What kind of mark?"

He hesitated, his jaw tightening as though weighing how much to tell her. "It's not visible," he said finally. "It's more like... a tether. A thread that binds you to them. And once it's there, you're part of their story."

The absurdity of his words clawed at her, demanding reason where none seemed to exist. "You're not making sense," she said, her voice sharpening with panic. "What story? What are you talking about?"

Eryx stepped closer, his wet boots sinking slightly into the mud. "You felt it, didn't you? When the melody started. The way it pulled at you, like it was meant for you."

Liora opened her mouth to deny it, but the words wouldn't come. She had felt it—an inexplicable tug at her chest, a sense that the haunting song was somehow calling her name. She hated the way her silence seemed to confirm his claim.

"Why me?" she whispered.

Eryx exhaled, glancing skyward as if the answer might be

written in the swirling storm clouds. "They choose people who are lost," he said. "People with nowhere to go, no one to miss them. They make it easy to follow."

"I wasn't going to follow them," she snapped, though her voice wavered.

"You don't have to," Eryx replied. "Once the tether is there, they'll come to you."

The wind howled, whipping her hair around her face. The shadows of the forest seemed to press closer, and Liora fought the urge to retreat further under the tree's gnarled branches. "How do you know all this?" she demanded, her voice rising. "How do you know what they are?"

Eryx's expression darkened, and for a moment, she thought he might refuse to answer. But then he spoke, his voice carrying a weight that sent another shiver down her spine. "Because I've been running from them for years."

The revelation landed like a blow, knocking the breath from her lungs. "What?" she asked, taking an involuntary step back. "You're part of it?"

"I was," he admitted. "But I escaped. At least, I thought I did." His gaze flickered to her, and she saw the shadow of regret in his eyes. "Now I'm not so sure."

The ground seemed to shift beneath her feet. The stranger who had pulled her from the road, the man who had claimed to mean her no harm, was tied to the same thing that now threatened her. And he had been hiding it all along.

"I should have kept walking," she muttered, her voice tight with anger. "I should have ignored you and kept walking."

"If you had," Eryx said quietly, "they would have taken you already."

His words froze her, cutting through her indignation like a knife. She clenched her fists, her nails biting into her palms. "So what now?" she demanded. "What am I supposed to do? Just wait for them to find me?"

"There's a way to fight it," he said. "But it's not simple. And it's not safe."

Liora laughed bitterly, the sound harsh against the storm. "Safe? You dragged me into this, and now you're worried about safe?"

Eryx didn't flinch at her anger. Instead, he met her gaze with a calm intensity that unnerved her. "You don't have to trust me," he said. "But if you want to survive this, you'll have to follow me."

"Follow you where?" she asked, though part of her was already bracing for the answer.

"To the Caravan," he said. "If we're going to break the tether, we have to go to the source."

The Eternal Caravan

Liora stared at him, her mind reeling. She wanted to argue, to scream at him for dragging her into this nightmare. But beneath the storm's fury, she couldn't ignore the truth that gnawed at the edges of her mind: he was the only one who seemed to understand what was happening. And if she wanted answers, she would have to stay close.

"Fine," she said finally, her voice shaking. "But if you're lying to me—"

"I'm not," Eryx said, cutting her off. "I have no reason to."

She studied him for a moment longer, searching his face for any hint of deception. All she found was a grim determination that mirrored her own fear.

"Then let's go," she said, her heart hammering against her ribs. "Before I change my mind."

Eryx nodded, turning toward the road. The storm seemed to ease as they began walking, the rain softening to a steady drizzle. But the melody lingered in the air, growing fainter with each step yet never truly disappearing.

As they walked, Liora found herself glancing over her shoulder, half expecting the shadowy figures to reappear. The road stretched endlessly before them, and though Eryx moved with purpose, she couldn't shake the feeling that they were walking into a trap.

"What is the Caravan?" she asked after a long silence. "What do they want?"

Eryx's jaw tightened, and for a moment, she thought he might not answer. But then he spoke, his voice low and haunted. "They're collectors," he said. "Of people, of stories, of souls. They wander forever, pulling others into their ranks. No one knows where they came from or why they exist. Only that once you're part of them, there's no going back."

Liora swallowed hard, her mouth dry despite the rain. "And you escaped?"

"Barely," he said. "And I've been looking for a way to break the cycle ever since."

The weight of his words settled heavily on her, but she couldn't bring herself to ask the question that lingered in her mind: What had it cost him to escape? And what would it cost her to do the same?

Ahead, the forest began to thin, and faint lights flickered in the distance. Liora's pulse quickened as she realized they were approaching a campsite. The smell of wood smoke and the faint sound of music drifted toward them, but it wasn't the haunting melody she had heard before. This was livelier, filled with laughter and the clink of mugs.

"The Caravan?" she asked, her voice barely above a whisper.

Eryx shook his head. "Not yet," he said. "But it's close."

The Eternal Caravan

Liora clenched her fists, her steps faltering as they neared the camp. The warmth of the firelight beckoned, but so did the lingering fear that they were walking into something far darker than she could imagine.

And somewhere in the distance, almost too faint to hear, the song of the Caravan played on.

Three

Whispers in the Wind

The campfire crackled in the center of the clearing, its flames casting flickering shadows against the towering trees that encircled the makeshift refuge. Liora sat on a weathered log, her damp clothes clinging to her skin and the chill of the night settling deep in her bones. The warmth of the fire barely touched her, though it was not the cold that made her shiver. It was the silence—the kind of silence that seemed to have a presence of its own, lingering in the spaces between the laughter and song of the strangers gathered around the flames.

The people in the camp seemed normal enough at first glance. Travelers, traders, perhaps drifters like herself, their faces illuminated by the golden glow of the firelight. Yet there was something unsettling about them. Their laughter was too easy, their smiles too wide, as though they were performing for an

The Eternal Caravan

unseen audience. Every now and then, one of them would glance toward the edge of the clearing, where the trees loomed like silent sentinels, and their laughter would falter.

Eryx sat a few feet away, his posture relaxed, but his eyes were sharp as they swept over the group. He had not spoken much since they arrived, offering only terse explanations when Liora pressed him for answers. She didn't trust him, not entirely, but for now, he was the only thread of understanding in this tangled web she had stumbled into.

A woman with auburn hair approached them, carrying two steaming bowls of stew. Her face was kind, but her eyes held a peculiar intensity as she handed the bowls to Liora and Eryx.

"You must be famished," she said, her voice smooth and lilting. "The storm has a way of draining the strength from travelers."

Liora accepted the bowl with a polite nod, though her stomach churned at the thought of eating. She glanced at Eryx, who merely murmured his thanks and set the bowl aside, untouched. The woman's gaze lingered on him for a moment, a flicker of recognition passing through her eyes before she turned and walked away.

"You're not eating?" Liora asked, her voice low.

Eryx shook his head, his expression unreadable. "Not hungry."

Liora frowned but said nothing. She lifted her spoon, letting the stew's rich aroma waft toward her. It smelled safe enough—

earthy and hearty, the kind of meal that would warm her from the inside out. But as the first drop touched her lips, a sudden unease gripped her. The taste was fine, but something about it felt wrong, as though it didn't belong to her.

She set the bowl down, her appetite evaporating. Eryx noticed and gave her a pointed look but didn't comment. Instead, he leaned closer, his voice barely above a whisper. "Don't let your guard down."

"Wasn't planning to," she muttered, glancing around the camp. The others were engrossed in their conversations, their laughter mingling with the crackle of the fire. Yet Liora couldn't shake the feeling that they were being watched.

The wind picked up, rustling the leaves overhead and sending a shiver down her spine. The sound seemed to carry a whisper, faint and fleeting, just on the edge of hearing. She turned her head, straining to catch it, but it was gone as quickly as it had come.

"Did you hear that?" she asked, her voice tight.

Eryx's eyes narrowed. "Hear what?"

"A whisper," she said. "In the wind."

He tensed, his gaze darting toward the trees. "Stay close to the fire," he said, his tone suddenly urgent.

"Why? What's out there?" Liora demanded, her voice rising

slightly.

Eryx didn't answer. Instead, he stood and moved toward the edge of the clearing, his movements slow and deliberate. Liora watched him, her unease growing with every step he took. The firelight cast long shadows across the ground, and for a moment, she thought she saw something move just beyond the circle of light.

She stood, her instincts screaming at her to stay where she was but her curiosity pulling her forward. "Eryx," she called softly, following him to the tree line. "What are you doing?"

"Listening," he said without turning around. His head tilted slightly, as though tuning in to a frequency only he could hear.

Liora stopped a few feet behind him, her gaze flickering between the dark forest and his rigid form. The whispers returned, clearer this time, though still indecipherable. They seemed to swirl around her, brushing against her ears like the ghost of a touch.

"Do you hear it now?" she asked, her voice barely audible.

"Yes," Eryx said, his voice tight. "They're closer than I thought."

"Who?" she demanded, her frustration bubbling to the surface. "You keep saying they, but I don't even know what we're dealing with!"

Eryx turned to face her, his expression grim. "The Caravan," he said. "This camp—it's a waypoint. A place they pass through, leaving traces behind."

Liora's stomach twisted. "You mean these people…?"

"They're not part of it," he said quickly. "Not yet. But they've been touched by it, just like you."

"Touched by what?" she pressed, her voice rising. "What is the Caravan? Why are they after us?"

Eryx sighed, running a hand through his damp hair. "The Caravan isn't just a group of travelers," he said. "It's a force. A story that pulls people in and binds them to its will. Once you're part of it, you can't escape. Not unless…"

"Not unless what?" she asked, her breath catching.

Before he could answer, the wind surged, carrying the whispers with it. The flames of the campfire danced wildly, casting distorted shadows that seemed to writhe and twist. The laughter of the camp died abruptly, replaced by an eerie silence. Liora turned to see the others staring at the fire, their expressions frozen in identical masks of fear.

"What's happening?" she whispered.

Eryx grabbed her arm, pulling her back toward the fire. "They're here."

The words sent a jolt of terror through her. She looked around frantically, searching for any sign of the figures she had seen on the road. The shadows seemed to shift and ripple, and for a moment, she thought she saw faces in the darkness—pale, hollow-eyed faces that watched her with an unsettling intensity.

The whispers grew louder, forming words she couldn't understand. They seemed to come from everywhere and nowhere, a chorus of voices weaving together in a haunting melody. Liora clapped her hands over her ears, but it did little to block out the sound.

"What do we do?" she asked, her voice trembling.

"Stay in the light," Eryx said, his grip on her arm tightening. "Whatever you do, don't leave the circle."

The fire roared suddenly, its flames leaping higher as if in defiance of the encroaching darkness. The others in the camp huddled closer, their fear palpable. Liora could feel the pull of the whispers, a strange, almost hypnotic sensation that made her want to step into the shadows. She fought against it, her breaths coming in short, panicked gasps.

"They're trying to draw you in," Eryx said, his voice steady despite the chaos around them. "You have to resist."

"I don't understand," she said, tears pricking her eyes. "Why me? Why is this happening?"

Eryx didn't answer. His focus was on the shadows, his body

tense and ready to move. The whispers reached a crescendo, and Liora thought she saw movement at the edge of the clearing—a figure stepping into the light, its features obscured by a hood.

The figure raised a hand, and the whispers ceased abruptly, leaving a deafening silence in their wake. The campfire dimmed, its flames shrinking to a feeble flicker. Liora's heart pounded in her chest as the figure lowered its hood, revealing a face she recognized—a face she had seen in her dreams.

"No," she whispered, her voice barely audible.

The figure smiled, its expression cold and knowing. "Welcome, Liora," it said, its voice a chilling echo. "We've been waiting for you."

Four

The Vanishing Map

The first light of dawn filtered through the dense canopy above, casting fragmented beams onto the muddy ground as the camp stirred to life. Liora sat by the dying embers of the campfire, her eyes fixed on the horizon. Her mind was a tangled web of fear, confusion, and questions that offered no answers. The events of the night before played on a loop in her head: the whispers, the shadowy figure that seemed to know her name, and the chilling smile that had frozen her blood.

Eryx had stayed close throughout the night, though he said little. Now, he crouched a few feet away, his cloak draped over his shoulders as he sharpened a blade with meticulous focus. The rhythmic scrape of stone against steel was oddly soothing, a tether to reality amidst the surreal nightmare that surrounded them.

"What happens now?" Liora finally asked, her voice breaking the fragile silence.

Eryx didn't look up. "We keep moving," he said. "The further we get from this place, the better."

"And go where?" she pressed. "You said the Caravan is everywhere. How do we escape something that's always moving?"

Eryx paused, his gaze lifting to meet hers. For a moment, she thought she saw a flicker of doubt in his eyes, but it was gone as quickly as it came. "There's a place," he said. "A safe haven. It's not easy to find, but if we can reach it, we'll have a chance."

"A chance at what?" she asked.

"To break the tether," he said simply.

The words hung between them, heavy with unspoken implications. Liora wanted to believe him, but doubt gnawed at her. The figure from the night before had known her name. How could she escape something that already seemed to have its claws in her?

Before she could voice her thoughts, a commotion erupted on the far side of the camp. Raised voices carried through the morning air, drawing the attention of everyone nearby. Liora and Eryx exchanged a tense glance before rising to their feet and making their way toward the source of the noise.

They found a small crowd gathered around a wiry man who was gesturing wildly, his face red with anger. In his hands, he clutched a rolled piece of parchment, which he waved in the air like a weapon.

"It's gone!" the man shouted. "I swear it was here last night!"

"Calm down, Elias," a woman said, her tone soothing but wary. "What's gone?"

"The map!" Elias snapped, unrolling the parchment and shoving it toward her. "Look! It's blank!"

The crowd murmured, their unease palpable. Liora edged closer, her curiosity piqued. Eryx stayed at her side, his expression grim as he observed the scene.

"What kind of map?" Liora asked, her voice cutting through the murmurs.

Elias turned to her, his eyes narrowing. "The only map that matters," he said. "The one that shows the way to—" He stopped abruptly, his gaze flicking to Eryx. "You. You know what I'm talking about, don't you?"

Eryx's jaw tightened. "What happened?" he asked, ignoring the question.

"I don't know!" Elias snapped, his frustration spilling over. "I checked it last night before the fire went out. It was there, clear as day. The path, the markings, everything. Now it's gone, like

The Vanishing Map

it was never there to begin with!"

He held the parchment out for them to see. Liora stepped closer, her eyes scanning the blank surface. There was nothing—no lines, no symbols, no indication that it had ever been a map. The parchment felt old, its edges worn and frayed, but it was utterly devoid of markings.

"It's not blank," Eryx said, his voice low.

Elias glared at him. "Are you blind? There's nothing there!"

"It's hidden," Eryx said. "The map isn't meant to be seen unless it wants to be."

The murmurs grew louder, the tension in the air thickening. "What does that mean?" someone demanded. "How can a map decide to disappear?"

Eryx ignored the question, his attention focused on Elias. "Where did you get this?"

Elias hesitated, his anger faltering under Eryx's piercing gaze. "It was… given to me," he admitted. "Years ago, by a traveler. He said it would guide me to what I seek, but only when the time was right."

"And now it's gone," Eryx said, his tone heavy with meaning. "Which means the time is no longer right."

Liora frowned, her mind racing. "Wait," she said, stepping forward. "If the map is tied to the Caravan, maybe it disappeared because of what happened last night. Maybe it's connected to—"

She broke off, the realization hitting her like a physical blow. "To me."

The crowd turned their attention to her, their expressions a mix of suspicion and curiosity. Eryx's gaze sharpened, his eyes narrowing as he studied her. "Explain," he said.

"The figure," Liora said, struggling to put her thoughts into words. "The one that appeared last night. It… it knew me. It said my name, like it was expecting me. What if that's why the map vanished? What if I'm the reason it's hidden?"

Elias snorted, crossing his arms. "That's ridiculous. How could you have anything to do with it?"

"I don't know," Liora admitted, her voice rising with frustration. "But isn't it too much of a coincidence? The map disappearing right after the Caravan showed up? Something's happening, and I'm part of it whether I want to be or not."

"She's right," Eryx said, cutting through the noise. "The map didn't vanish—it's reacting. To her, to the tether, to everything that's happening. The question isn't why it's gone. The question is how we bring it back."

The crowd fell silent, the weight of his words settling over them. Liora's pulse quickened as she looked at Eryx, a flicker of hope mingling with her fear. "How do we do that?" she asked.

Eryx's expression darkened. "The map is tied to the Caravan," he said. "If we want to retrieve it, we'll have to follow their trail."

A ripple of unease passed through the crowd. "Follow them?" someone said, their voice shaking. "Are you mad? That's suicide!"

"It's the only way," Eryx said firmly. "The map is our best chance of finding the safe haven. Without it, we're lost."

Liora looked at him, her resolve hardening. "Then we follow the trail," she said. "Whatever it takes."

Eryx nodded, a glimmer of approval in his eyes. "We leave at dusk," he said. "The Caravan moves at night, and so will we."

The crowd began to disperse, their murmurs fading as they returned to their tasks. Elias lingered, his gaze fixed on the blank parchment in his hands. "You'd better be right about this," he muttered, before stalking away.

Liora turned to Eryx, her heart pounding. "Are we really doing this?" she asked.

"We don't have a choice," he said. "The map disappeared for a reason. If we want answers, we have to go to the source."

She nodded, though fear coiled in her stomach like a living

thing. The whispers from the night before still haunted her, a reminder of the danger they faced. But as the day wore on and the light began to fade, she steeled herself for what was to come.

When dusk fell, the two of them set out, the blank parchment tucked safely in Eryx's satchel. The forest closed in around them, its shadows deepening with every step. And somewhere in the distance, the haunting melody of the Caravan began to play, a siren's song leading them into the unknown.

Five

A Thread Between Us

The melody of the Caravan wove through the night like an ethereal thread, faint and haunting yet impossibly clear against the hushed sounds of the forest. It seemed to dance on the edges of Liora's awareness, pulling her forward even as every instinct screamed for her to turn back. The darkness felt alive, the trees whispering secrets she couldn't quite hear, their gnarled branches twisting like skeletal hands reaching for her.

Eryx walked a few steps ahead, his movements purposeful but silent. The blank map was tucked securely in his satchel, a weight that seemed heavier than parchment could justify. Liora followed closely, her eyes darting to every shadow, her heart pounding with a rhythm that matched the distant, unearthly tune.

"Does it ever stop?" she asked, her voice barely a whisper.

Eryx glanced over his shoulder, his face unreadable in the dim moonlight. "The song?" he asked. "No. It doesn't stop. You just get used to it."

Liora's lips tightened. The idea of getting used to something so unnatural made her stomach twist. She quickened her pace until she was walking beside him, her steps matching his. "You said the Caravan is always moving," she said. "If that's true, how do we follow something that doesn't leave a trail?"

Eryx hesitated, his eyes scanning the darkened forest ahead. "They leave more than a trail," he said finally. "They leave echoes. Fragments of their presence, like threads that weave through time and space. If you know how to look, you can follow them."

"Threads?" Liora repeated, frowning. "What kind of threads?"

"You've already felt them," he said, his voice low. "The pull you felt when you heard the song—that's one of them. It's subtle, but it's there."

Liora opened her mouth to argue, but the truth of his words silenced her. She had felt something—a faint tug at her very core, as though the song had wrapped itself around her like an invisible thread. The thought sent a shiver down her spine.

They continued in silence for a while, the only sounds the rustle of leaves beneath their boots and the faint melody that seemed to grow louder with every step. Liora's mind churned with questions, but the oppressive weight of the night kept her from voicing them. She focused on the path ahead, on the faint glow of the moon filtering through the trees, on the steady rhythm of Eryx's steps.

Then she saw it.

At first, she thought it was a trick of the light, a fleeting glimmer that disappeared as quickly as it had appeared. But as they moved deeper into the forest, the glimmers grew more frequent, more distinct. Thin strands of silvery light crisscrossed the air around them, like the gossamer threads of a spider's web. They seemed to pulse faintly, as though alive, their soft glow casting eerie patterns on the ground.

"What... what is this?" Liora whispered, her voice trembling.

"The threads," Eryx said, his tone matter-of-fact. "They're stronger here. It means we're getting closer."

Liora reached out hesitantly, her fingers brushing against one of the strands. The moment she made contact, a jolt of sensation shot through her—a kaleidoscope of images, sounds, and emotions that left her gasping. She snatched her hand back, her heart racing.

"Don't touch them," Eryx said sharply, grabbing her wrist before she could reach for another. "They're not meant for you."

"What was that?" she asked, her voice shaking.

"They're memories," he said. "Fragments of the lives the Caravan has claimed. If you touch them, you'll feel what they felt, see what they saw. But it's not meant for you. It's dangerous."

Liora nodded, her fingers curling into fists as she resisted the urge to reach out again. The threads seemed to hum faintly, as though responding to her presence, and she couldn't shake the feeling that they were watching her.

"Why can't I stop feeling them?" she asked, her voice barely audible. "It's like they're pulling me in."

Eryx's grip on her wrist tightened briefly before he let go. "Because you're tethered," he said. "The threads are connected to you now. They want you to follow."

The words sent a chill down her spine. She rubbed her wrist absently, her gaze fixed on the glowing threads that surrounded them. "And you?" she asked. "Are you tethered, too?"

Eryx hesitated, his eyes darkening. "I was," he said. "But I broke free. Or at least, I thought I did."

Liora frowned, her thoughts racing. "How did you break free?"

His jaw tightened. "It doesn't matter."

"It matters to me," she said, her voice rising. "If you know how to escape this, I need to know. I didn't ask for any of this. I didn't ask to be part of their—"

She broke off abruptly, her breath catching in her throat. One of the threads had shifted, moving toward her like a snake uncoiling. She stumbled back, her pulse racing as the thread hovered inches from her face.

"Don't move," Eryx said, his voice low and urgent. "Just stay still."

Liora froze, her heart hammering as the thread pulsed faintly, its glow illuminating her face. It seemed to examine her, as though deciding what to do. Then, slowly, it wrapped itself around her wrist, its silvery light sinking into her skin. The sensation was overwhelming—a flood of emotions and memories that weren't her own, a cacophony of voices and images that threatened to drown her.

"Liora!" Eryx's voice cut through the chaos, sharp and commanding. "Focus on me. Look at me."

She forced her eyes to meet his, anchoring herself to his steady gaze. The flood of sensations began to recede, leaving her breathless and trembling. The thread released her wrist and drifted away, its glow fading as it disappeared into the darkness.

"What just happened?" she asked, her voice shaking.

Eryx's expression was grim. "It marked you," he said. "It's part of the tether. They're drawing you in."

"What does that mean?" she demanded, panic creeping into her voice. "What happens now?"

"It means you're more connected to them than ever," he said. "And if we don't reach the safe haven soon, they'll claim you."

Liora swallowed hard, the weight of his words sinking in. She looked down at her wrist, where the thread had touched her. The skin was unmarked, but she could still feel its presence, a faint hum that resonated deep within her.

"We need to keep moving," Eryx said, his voice firm. "The longer we stay here, the stronger the threads will get."

Liora nodded, her fear giving way to determination. She fell into step beside him, her eyes scanning the forest for any sign of movement. The threads continued to glimmer around them, their soft light casting an otherworldly glow on the path ahead.

As they walked, Liora couldn't shake the feeling that the threads were alive, that they were watching her, guiding her. And somewhere in the distance, the melody of the Caravan played on, a siren's song that called to her with every step.

By the time the first light of dawn began to break through the trees, Liora felt as though she were walking a tightrope, balanced precariously between the world she knew and the one that was pulling her in. She glanced at Eryx, his face shadowed but resolute, and felt the faintest flicker of hope.

Whatever lay ahead, she wasn't facing it alone. But as the whispers of the threads echoed in her mind, she couldn't help but wonder: was that enough to keep her tethered to herself?

Six

The Woman in the Cloak

The road ahead was nothing more than a narrow trail, its edges blurred by the thick mist that hung low over the forest floor. The rising sun was veiled behind a shroud of gray clouds, casting the world in muted shades of silver and green. Liora followed closely behind Eryx, her senses on high alert. The faint melody of the Caravan had faded into the distance, but its absence was no comfort. It left behind an oppressive silence, broken only by the soft crunch of leaves beneath their boots.

Her wrist still tingled where the thread had touched her the night before, and she found herself rubbing the spot absently, as though trying to erase the memory of it. The sensation wasn't painful, but it was persistent—a faint hum that seemed to resonate deep within her.

The Eternal Caravan

"We'll stop here," Eryx said abruptly, his voice cutting through the stillness. He gestured to a small clearing just off the path, bordered by a dense thicket of ferns. "It's as good a place as any."

Liora glanced around, unease prickling at her skin. "Why are we stopping?" she asked.

"We need rest," he said, lowering his satchel to the ground. "And we need to talk."

The way he said it made her stomach tighten. She sat down on a fallen log, watching as Eryx rummaged through his satchel and pulled out the blank map. He unrolled it carefully, spreading it across the ground. It was still as featureless as it had been the night before, its surface a pale, empty expanse that seemed to mock them.

"Any ideas?" she asked, her tone sharper than she intended.

Eryx ignored her question, his eyes fixed on the map. He traced a finger along its surface, his brow furrowed in concentration. "It's reacting to you," he said finally. "But not enough to reveal itself."

"What does that even mean?" she asked, frustration bubbling to the surface. "Why would a map react to me? I don't know anything about this world, or the Caravan, or—"

She broke off as a faint rustling reached her ears. It was a subtle sound, easily mistaken for the wind stirring the leaves, but it set her nerves on edge. She looked around, her hand instinctively going to the knife she had tucked into her belt.

"Did you hear that?" she whispered.

Eryx looked up sharply, his posture tensing. He stood, his gaze scanning the trees. "Stay close," he said, his voice low.

The rustling grew louder, accompanied by the faint crunch of footsteps. Liora's grip tightened on the hilt of her knife as she rose to her feet, her heart pounding. The sound came from the direction of the path, growing steadily closer until a figure emerged from the mist.

It was a woman, her face obscured by the hood of a long, dark cloak. She moved with a graceful, almost ethereal quality, her steps barely disturbing the leaves beneath her feet. The sight of her sent a chill down Liora's spine, though she couldn't say why. There was nothing overtly threatening about the woman, yet every instinct screamed that she was dangerous.

"Who are you?" Eryx demanded, stepping forward to place himself between Liora and the stranger.

The woman stopped a few paces away, her head tilting slightly as she regarded him. "A friend," she said, her voice smooth and melodic. "Or perhaps an enemy, depending on how you choose to see me."

"Not an answer," Eryx said, his hand hovering near the hilt of his sword. "What do you want?"

The woman chuckled softly, a sound that sent shivers down Liora's spine. "What I want is irrelevant," she said. "What matters is what she wants."

She turned her gaze to Liora, and for the first time, Liora saw her face clearly. The woman was beautiful in an otherworldly way, her features sharp and elegant, her eyes a piercing shade of green that seemed to see straight through her. But there was something unsettling about her beauty, a coldness that made it impossible to look away.

"I don't know what you mean," Liora said, forcing herself to meet the woman's gaze. "I didn't ask for any of this."

"Perhaps not," the woman said. "But the threads don't choose lightly. You're here for a reason, whether you realize it or not."

Liora glanced at Eryx, hoping for some kind of explanation, but his expression was unreadable. "What do you know about the threads?" she asked, her voice steady despite the fear clawing at her insides.

"I know enough," the woman said. "Enough to warn you."

"Warn me about what?" Liora asked.

"About him," the woman said, nodding toward Eryx. "You think he's your ally, but he's not telling you everything."

Liora frowned, her grip on her knife tightening. "What are you talking about?"

The Woman in the Cloak

The woman's smile was enigmatic, her eyes never leaving Liora's. "Ask him," she said. "Ask him what he did to escape the Caravan. Ask him what it cost."

Liora turned to Eryx, her heart sinking at the sudden tension in his expression. "What is she talking about?" she demanded. "What did you do?"

Eryx's jaw tightened, but he didn't respond. The silence stretched between them, heavy and suffocating.

"Go ahead," the woman said, her tone almost playful. "Tell her the truth. Or would you rather I do it for you?"

"That's enough," Eryx said sharply, his voice cutting through the air like a blade. He stepped toward the woman, his eyes blazing with fury. "You have no right—"

"No right?" the woman interrupted, her voice suddenly cold. "I have every right. You think you can run from the past, Eryx? It will catch up to you. It always does."

Eryx's hand went to his sword, but the woman didn't flinch. Instead, she stepped closer, her gaze locked on his. "You're walking a dangerous path," she said softly. "And you're dragging her with you."

"I'm protecting her," Eryx said through gritted teeth.

"Are you?" the woman asked, her voice laced with doubt. "Or are you just protecting yourself?"

Liora felt as though the ground had been pulled out from under her. She looked between them, her mind racing. "What is she talking about?" she asked, her voice rising. "Eryx, what's going on?"

Eryx didn't answer. His focus was entirely on the woman, his body tense and ready to strike. The woman smiled faintly, as though she had already won.

"You have a choice, Liora," she said, her gaze shifting back to her. "You can follow him and trust that he has your best interests at heart. Or you can listen to the threads. They won't lie to you."

Before Liora could respond, the woman stepped back into the mist, her cloak billowing around her like smoke. Within seconds, she was gone, leaving nothing but the faint scent of wildflowers in her wake.

Liora turned to Eryx, her anger bubbling over. "Who was she?" she demanded. "And what did she mean about you not telling me everything?"

Eryx sighed, running a hand through his hair. "She's part of the Caravan," he said reluctantly. "A messenger. She exists to sow doubt, to make you question everything."

"And should I be questioning you?" Liora asked, her voice trembling.

Eryx hesitated, his eyes meeting hers. "You have every right to," he said quietly. "But right now, you need to trust me. If we're going to survive this, we have to keep moving."

Liora stared at him, torn between anger and fear. The woman's words echoed in her mind, filling her with doubt. But as she glanced at the trees, the memory of the threads and the haunting melody reminded her of the danger that lurked in the shadows.

For now, she had no choice but to follow him. But the seed of doubt had been planted, and she couldn't shake the feeling that her trust in Eryx might cost her more than she was willing to lose.

Seven

Threads of Yesterday

The forest seemed to grow darker as the day wore on, the dense canopy overhead blotting out what little sunlight remained. Liora walked in silence, her thoughts a tangle of fear, frustration, and questions she couldn't yet articulate. Eryx moved ahead of her, his strides purposeful, but she noticed the tension in his shoulders, the way his hand rested a little too often on the hilt of his sword.

The woman in the cloak had left more than just unease in her wake. She had left a shadow—a lingering doubt that clung to Liora like the mist rising from the forest floor. She glanced down at her wrist, where the invisible thread from the Caravan had left its mark. The spot still tingled faintly, as though it were a beacon calling to something unseen.

"Do you even know where we're going?" she asked, her voice

breaking the heavy silence.

Eryx didn't turn around. "Yes."

"That's not an answer," Liora pressed, quickening her pace to catch up to him. "You said the map reacts to me, but it's still blank. How do you know we're not just wandering in circles?"

Eryx stopped abruptly, and Liora nearly collided with him. He turned to face her, his expression unreadable. "Because the threads are leading us," he said. "Can't you feel it?"

Liora hesitated. She didn't want to admit it, but she could feel something—a faint pull, like an invisible current nudging her forward. It wasn't constant, but every now and then, it would surge, guiding her steps in subtle, inexplicable ways.

"I feel… something," she said reluctantly. "But that doesn't mean I trust it."

"You don't have to trust it," Eryx said. "You just have to follow it."

"That's easy for you to say," she snapped. "You're not the one it's marked."

Eryx's eyes darkened, but he didn't respond. Instead, he turned and resumed walking, leaving Liora fuming in his wake. She followed him, her anger simmering just beneath the surface.

As they walked, the forest began to change. The trees grew

taller and closer together, their twisted branches forming an almost impenetrable wall on either side of the path. The air grew heavier, thick with the scent of damp earth and decaying leaves. Liora felt a growing sense of unease, as though the forest itself were alive and watching her.

It wasn't long before the threads began to appear again. Thin, silvery strands stretched between the trees, their faint glow casting eerie patterns on the ground. Liora avoided looking directly at them, afraid of what she might see if she stared too long. But the threads seemed to pulse faintly, as though they were aware of her presence.

"What are these things?" she asked, her voice barely above a whisper. "You said they're memories, but whose? Are they from the Caravan?"

Eryx glanced back at her, his expression grim. "They're from everyone the Caravan has touched," he said. "Every life it's taken, every story it's consumed. The threads are all that's left of them."

Liora shuddered, her gaze flicking to the glowing strands. "Why are they still here? If the Caravan moves, why don't the threads disappear with it?"

"Because they're not tied to the Caravan's location," Eryx said. "They're tied to its influence. Wherever the Caravan has been, the threads remain."

Liora fell silent, the weight of his words settling over her like a heavy blanket. The thought of all those lives, all those stories trapped in the threads, was almost too much to bear. She couldn't shake the feeling that she was walking through a graveyard, the air thick with the ghosts of the past.

It wasn't long before the threads began to change. They grew thicker and more numerous, their glow brighter and more intense. Liora felt the pull grow stronger, a persistent tug that seemed to resonate deep within her. She tried to ignore it, but the sensation was impossible to shake.

"Do you feel that?" she asked, her voice trembling.

Eryx nodded, his jaw clenched. "We're close."

"Close to what?" Liora demanded. "What's happening?"

Before Eryx could answer, the pull surged, and Liora stumbled forward, her breath catching in her throat. The world around her seemed to blur, the threads weaving together into a shimmering tapestry that pulsed with light. She closed her eyes, but the light was still there, burning behind her eyelids.

And then the memories came.

It was like a floodgate had opened, a torrent of images and emotions crashing over her. She saw faces she didn't recognize, heard voices speaking words she didn't understand. There was pain and joy, love and loss, all blending together in a chaotic symphony that left her gasping for air.

The Eternal Caravan

She saw a woman with dark hair and piercing eyes, her face twisted in anguish as she reached out to someone just out of sight. She saw a man standing in the rain, his shoulders slumped in defeat as the Caravan's melody played in the background. She saw a child clutching a thread, its glow fading as tears streamed down their face.

And then she saw herself.

Liora was standing in a field, the sky above her painted in shades of crimson and gold. The Caravan was there, its shadowy figures moving in unison as the melody filled the air. She felt the thread around her wrist tighten, pulling her forward, and she saw Eryx standing at the edge of the field, his face etched with pain.

"Liora!" His voice cut through the chaos, pulling her back to the present.

She opened her eyes, her breath coming in ragged gasps. The threads were still there, but the tapestry had unraveled, leaving only faint traces of light. Eryx was standing in front of her, his hands on her shoulders, his expression a mix of concern and anger.

"What happened?" he demanded.

"I don't know," she said, her voice shaking. "I saw... things. Memories, I think. But they weren't mine. At least, I don't think they were."

Eryx's grip on her shoulders tightened. "What did you see?"

She hesitated, the images still fresh in her mind. "I saw the Caravan," she said finally. "And I saw myself. But it wasn't me. It was like… I was part of it."

Eryx's expression darkened, and he released her shoulders, stepping back. "It's stronger than I thought," he said, almost to himself. "The threads are pulling you deeper."

"What does that mean?" Liora asked, her fear rising. "Am I… becoming one of them?"

"Not yet," Eryx said. "But if we don't find the safe haven soon, you will be."

The words hit her like a punch to the gut, leaving her breathless. She looked down at her wrist, where the thread had marked her, and felt a surge of panic. "What do we do?" she asked, her voice barely above a whisper.

"We keep moving," Eryx said firmly. "And we don't stop until we find the safe haven. Whatever it takes."

Liora nodded, her resolve hardening. She didn't know what the future held, but one thing was certain: she couldn't let the Caravan claim her. Not without a fight.

As they resumed their journey, the threads continued to shimmer around them, their glow a constant reminder of the danger that lay ahead. And somewhere in the distance, the faint melody of the Caravan played on, a haunting reminder that time was running out.

Eight

The Forbidden Dance

The clearing was alive with sound and light, a stark contrast to the eerie quiet of the forest they had left behind. Torches burned brightly, their golden flames casting long, dancing shadows over the gathering of people. Liora stood at the edge of the crowd, her heart pounding as she took in the scene before her. The celebration was in full swing, a chaotic blend of music, laughter, and movement that seemed almost too vibrant to be real.

Eryx stood beside her, his posture tense and his eyes scanning the crowd. "This is wrong," he muttered under his breath.

"What do you mean?" Liora asked, her voice barely audible over the music.

"This isn't a normal gathering," he said. "It's a lure."

Liora frowned, her gaze shifting to the dancers who moved in perfect harmony to the rhythm of the music. Their movements were fluid and mesmerizing, each step precise yet effortless. It was beautiful, but there was something unsettling about it—something that made her skin prickle with unease.

"They don't look dangerous," she said, though the words sounded hollow even to her.

Eryx shook his head. "It's not them you should be afraid of. It's the dance."

Before Liora could ask what he meant, a tall man with a commanding presence stepped into the center of the clearing. He wore a dark cloak trimmed with silver, and his face was partially obscured by a mask that glimmered in the firelight. The crowd fell silent as he raised his arms, his voice cutting through the air with unnatural clarity.

"Welcome, travelers," he said, his tone rich and inviting. "Tonight, we celebrate the Threaded Moon—a night of unity, a night of remembrance. Join us in the dance, and let the threads weave their story."

The crowd erupted into cheers, and the music resumed, louder and more fervent than before. Liora felt a strange pull, an almost magnetic urge to step forward and join the dancers. She gripped Eryx's arm, her fingers digging into his sleeve. "What's happening?" she asked, her voice trembling.

"It's the song," Eryx said, his expression grim. "It's designed to draw you in. You have to resist it."

"But why?" she pressed. "What happens if I don't?"

Eryx hesitated, his gaze darkening. "The dance isn't just a celebration," he said. "It's a binding ritual. Once you join, you become part of the Caravan."

The words sent a chill down her spine. She took a step back, her grip on Eryx tightening. "Then why are we here?" she demanded. "Why didn't we just avoid this place?"

"Because the threads led us here," he said. "And if we're going to break your tether, we need to understand why."

Liora's stomach twisted, but she nodded, her resolve hardening. She wouldn't let the Caravan claim her—not without a fight.

As the music swelled, the dancers began to form a circle, their movements growing more intricate and synchronized. The air seemed to hum with energy, and the threads that had been faint and distant were now vivid and tangible, weaving through the crowd like living things. Liora felt the pull intensify, the invisible thread around her wrist tightening as if urging her forward.

"Liora," Eryx said sharply, his voice snapping her out of the trance. "Stay with me."

She nodded, her heart racing as she fought to resist the pull. But as the dance continued, she noticed something strange.

The Eternal Caravan

The threads weren't just weaving through the crowd—they were converging on her.

"Eryx," she said, her voice shaking. "Something's happening."

He followed her gaze, his eyes narrowing as he saw the threads. "They're targeting you," he said. "They know you're here."

"What do we do?" she asked, panic rising in her chest.

Eryx didn't answer immediately. He seemed to be weighing his options, his jaw tight with tension. "We can't run," he said finally. "Not yet. They'll know."

"Know what?" she demanded.

"That you're resisting," he said. "If they realize you're trying to escape, they'll tighten the tether. Right now, we need to blend in."

"Blend in?" she repeated, incredulous. "You just said the dance is a binding ritual!"

"I know," he said. "But if we don't join, they'll know we don't belong. We'll have to be careful, but it's the only way."

Liora hesitated, her fear warring with the urgency in his voice. Finally, she nodded, though every instinct screamed at her to run. "Fine," she said. "But if I get bound to the Caravan, I'm holding you responsible."

Eryx's lips quirked in a faint, humorless smile. "I wouldn't expect anything less."

They stepped into the circle, their movements hesitant at first. The threads seemed to respond immediately, weaving around them with a renewed intensity. Liora felt the pull grow stronger, but she forced herself to focus on the music, matching her steps to the rhythm.

The dance was unlike anything she had ever experienced. It was both fluid and rigid, the movements dictated by the threads that guided her steps. She felt a strange connection to the others in the circle, as though they were all part of the same intricate web. The sensation was intoxicating, and for a moment, she forgot why she was resisting.

"Liora," Eryx said, his voice low and urgent. "Don't let it take you."

She looked at him, his face drawn and serious. The reminder snapped her out of the trance, and she nodded, focusing on the thread that bound her wrist. She could feel it pulsing faintly, its energy growing with every step she took.

As the dance reached its peak, the masked man stepped forward again, his arms raised high. "The Threaded Moon binds us all," he declared. "Through the dance, we are one."

The threads around Liora surged, their light intensifying as they wove tighter around her. She felt a sharp tug, as though something was trying to pull her out of herself. She gasped,

The Eternal Caravan

her vision blurring as the world tilted around her.

"Eryx!" she cried, panic flooding her voice.

He was at her side in an instant, his hand gripping her arm. "Stay with me," he said. "Focus on me."

She clung to his voice, anchoring herself to the sound. Slowly, the pull began to weaken, the threads loosening their hold. The masked man turned toward her, his gaze locking onto hers. For a moment, she thought she saw recognition in his eyes.

"Enough," Eryx said, his voice cold and commanding. "We're leaving."

The masked man tilted his head, his expression unreadable behind the glittering mask. "The dance is not over," he said. "You cannot leave."

"Watch us," Eryx said, his tone daring him to intervene.

The man didn't move, but the threads around them began to shift, their glow dimming as the music faltered. Liora felt the pull weaken further, and she took a shaky step back, her breath coming in ragged gasps.

Eryx guided her out of the circle, his grip firm and steady. As they left the clearing, the music faded, and the forest swallowed them once more. Liora's heart pounded in her chest, the memory of the threads and the dance still fresh in her mind.

The Forbidden Dance

"What was that?" she asked, her voice trembling.

"A warning," Eryx said. "They know you're trying to break free. And they're not going to let you go easily."

Liora shivered, the weight of his words settling over her like a shadow. She looked back toward the clearing, but the light of the torches was already gone, swallowed by the darkness.

The dance was over, but the danger was far from past. The threads had tightened their grip, and the Caravan was closer than ever.

Nine

The First Betrayal

The forest closed in around them as Liora and Eryx pressed onward, their steps quick and silent. The remnants of the forbidden dance lingered in Liora's mind, vivid and haunting. Every thread that had wrapped around her wrist, every pulse of energy that had drawn her deeper into the Caravan's web—it all replayed in her thoughts like a sinister echo.

The air felt heavier now, as though the trees themselves were conspiring against their escape. Liora glanced over her shoulder, half-expecting to see the masked man or one of the dancers following them, but the path remained empty, shrouded in mist. Still, the sensation of being watched refused to leave her.

"We need to stop," she said, her voice trembling slightly. "Just for a minute."

Eryx turned to her, his face shadowed but his eyes sharp. "Stopping now would be a mistake."

"I can't keep going like this," she said, trying to steady her breathing. "I need to catch my breath."

He hesitated, his jaw tightening as he weighed her words. Finally, he nodded and gestured to a hollow between two massive trees. "We'll rest there. But not for long."

They moved into the hollow, and Liora sank onto a fallen log, her muscles aching from the relentless pace. She rubbed her wrist absently, the spot where the thread had wrapped around her still tingling. Eryx stood a few feet away, his posture rigid as he scanned the forest.

"What happened back there?" she asked, breaking the silence. "At the dance?"

"You felt it, didn't you?" he said, his voice low. "The threads pulling you in?"

Liora nodded. "It was like they were trying to... take something from me. Or maybe give me something. I don't know."

"That's how it starts," Eryx said. "The threads don't just connect you to the Caravan. They strip you of yourself piece by piece, until there's nothing left but the story they want you to be a part of."

"And what story is that?" she pressed.

Eryx's gaze flicked to her, his expression unreadable. "One you don't want to be in."

The cryptic answer frustrated her, but before she could press him further, the sound of rustling leaves reached her ears. She froze, her heart leaping into her throat. Eryx's hand went to his sword, his body tensing as he scanned the shadows.

"Stay here," he said, his voice a whisper.

"No way," she hissed, rising to her feet. "If something's out there, I'm not sitting here like a target."

He shot her a warning look but didn't argue. Instead, he moved silently toward the edge of the hollow, his sword drawn. Liora followed, her knife clutched tightly in her hand.

The rustling grew louder, accompanied by the faint crunch of footsteps. Liora's pulse quickened as the shadows shifted, and a figure emerged from the mist. It was a man, his clothes torn and his face streaked with dirt. He stumbled toward them, his eyes wide with panic.

"Help me," he gasped, collapsing to his knees. "Please, you have to help me."

Eryx didn't lower his sword. "Who are you?" he demanded.

"My name's Darian," the man said, his voice trembling. "I was at the dance. I... I tried to leave, but they wouldn't let me. I barely escaped."

Liora exchanged a glance with Eryx, her instincts screaming that something wasn't right. "How did you find us?" she asked.

Darian hesitated, his gaze flicking between them. "I followed the threads," he said finally. "They... they led me here."

"That's impossible," Eryx said, his voice cold. "The threads don't lead to freedom. They only lead to the Caravan."

"I'm telling the truth!" Darian insisted, his voice rising. "Please, you have to believe me. I don't want to go back."

Liora's grip on her knife tightened as doubt crept into her mind. The man's desperation seemed genuine, but Eryx's skepticism made her wary. "What do you think?" she asked Eryx.

"I think he's lying," Eryx said bluntly. "No one escapes the dance without a reason. And no one follows the threads here unless they're sent."

Darian's eyes widened in fear. "I'm not lying," he said. "I swear. I just want to be free."

"Then you'd better start explaining how you got here," Eryx said, his sword still pointed at the man's chest.

Darian opened his mouth to respond, but before he could speak, the threads began to appear. They shimmered faintly in the air, weaving through the trees and wrapping around Darian's body like ghostly tendrils. Liora took a step back, her breath catching in her throat.

"What's happening?" she whispered.

"It's a trap," Eryx said, his voice grim. "He's the bait."

As if on cue, the threads tightened around Darian, pulling him to his feet. His expression twisted with fear and pain as he struggled against their hold. "No!" he cried. "I didn't mean to—"

The words were cut off as the threads yanked him backward, dragging him into the shadows. Liora's heart raced as she watched him disappear, the forest swallowing him whole. The threads lingered for a moment longer, their light pulsing ominously, before vanishing into the darkness.

"We need to move," Eryx said, grabbing her arm and pulling her away from the hollow. "Now."

Liora followed him, her mind reeling. "What just happened?" she asked. "Was he… part of the Caravan?"

"He was already claimed," Eryx said. "The Caravan sent him to lure us in."

"But why?" she pressed. "What do they want from us?"

"You," Eryx said simply. "They want you."

The First Betrayal

The words hit her like a punch to the gut, leaving her breathless. She stumbled over a root, but Eryx caught her arm and steadied her. "Why me?" she asked, her voice barely audible.

"Because you're still resisting," he said. "And they don't like it when people resist."

The realization sent a chill down her spine. She glanced over her shoulder, half-expecting to see the threads chasing them, but the forest remained eerily still. "What do we do now?" she asked.

"We keep moving," Eryx said. "And we don't stop until we're out of their reach."

Liora nodded, her fear giving way to determination. She wouldn't let the Caravan claim her—not without a fight. But as they pushed deeper into the forest, the memory of Darian's terrified face lingered in her mind, a stark reminder of the danger that lay ahead.

And somewhere in the distance, the faint melody of the Caravan began to play again, its haunting tune a chilling promise that the threads were far from finished with them.

Ten

The Marked Book

The forest was an oppressive maze of twisted branches and creeping mist, each shadow a potential threat. Liora's legs burned with the effort of keeping pace with Eryx, but she refused to complain. She had no intention of slowing him down, not when the Caravan's haunting melody still echoed faintly in the distance.

They had been walking for hours when the terrain began to change. The dense forest gave way to a clearing, and in the center stood an abandoned building—a crumbling structure of stone and wood that seemed impossibly out of place. The roof was partially collapsed, and ivy crept up the walls, its tendrils snaking through cracks like veins feeding a dying heart.

Eryx stopped, his eyes narrowing as he studied the structure. "We'll rest here," he said.

The Marked Book

Liora eyed the building warily. "You think it's safe?"

"Safer than staying out here," he said, already moving toward the door. "The Caravan rarely lingers near places like this."

She followed him, her unease growing as they approached. The air around the building felt heavy, charged with a strange energy that made her skin prickle. The door creaked loudly as Eryx pushed it open, revealing an interior that was just as decayed as the exterior. Dust coated every surface, and the air was thick with the smell of damp wood and mildew.

They stepped inside, their footsteps echoing in the empty space. The room was sparsely furnished, with only a few broken chairs and a table that leaned precariously to one side. Shelves lined the walls, their contents long since looted or destroyed, but one shelf remained mostly intact, its dusty tomes still standing in neat rows.

Liora's gaze was drawn to the books immediately. Something about them seemed wrong, though she couldn't say why. She moved closer, her fingers brushing against the spines as she scanned the titles. Most were unreadable, their covers worn and faded, but one book stood out. It was larger than the others, its leather cover embossed with intricate designs that shimmered faintly in the dim light.

"What is this?" she murmured, pulling the book from the shelf.

Eryx turned, his eyes narrowing as he saw what she held. "Put it back."

"Why?" she asked, though her fingers tightened around the book instinctively. "It's just a book."

"It's not just a book," he said, his tone sharp. "It's a relic. The Caravan leaves them behind to mark the places they've been."

Liora hesitated, her curiosity battling with the warning in his voice. She opened the book, its pages brittle and yellowed with age. The writing inside was unlike anything she had ever seen—symbols and markings that seemed to shift and twist as she looked at them.

"What does it say?" she asked, her voice barely above a whisper.

"I don't know," Eryx said, moving closer. "And you don't want to find out. Those books are dangerous. They're tied to the threads."

Liora glanced at him, her heart racing. "What kind of danger are we talking about?"

"They're traps," he said. "The Caravan uses them to lure people in, to feed their curiosity until it consumes them."

The words sent a chill down her spine, but she couldn't bring herself to put the book down. There was something compelling about it, something that felt… familiar. She turned the page, her eyes scanning the strange symbols until they landed on an image—a detailed drawing of a figure bound in threads, their face obscured by a hood.

She gasped, the book slipping from her hands and landing on the floor with a dull thud. "That's me," she whispered, stepping back.

Eryx frowned, his gaze flicking to the book. He picked it up carefully, his eyes narrowing as he studied the page. "It's not you," he said after a moment. "But it's someone like you."

"What does that mean?" she asked, her voice trembling.

"It means the Caravan has been doing this for a long time," he said. "You're not the first person they've marked, and you won't be the last."

Liora's stomach twisted, a sick feeling settling in her chest. She wanted to look away, to distance herself from the book and everything it represented, but her eyes were drawn to the page like a moth to a flame. The figure in the drawing seemed to stare back at her, its faceless form a haunting mirror of her own fear.

"There's more," Eryx said, turning the page. The next image showed the same figure, but now they were surrounded by others—shadowy figures with threads wrapped around their wrists, pulling them closer.

"What are they doing?" Liora asked, her voice barely audible.

"They're becoming part of the Caravan," Eryx said grimly. "The threads bind them to the story, and once they're part of it, they can't escape."

Liora felt a wave of nausea, her knees threatening to give out. "Why would they leave something like this behind?" she asked. "Why show people what they're doing?"

"Because it's not just a warning," Eryx said. "It's an invitation. The Caravan thrives on curiosity. The more you try to understand it, the more you're drawn in."

She took a shaky step back, her hands trembling. "We need to destroy it," she said. "We can't just leave it here."

Eryx shook his head. "You can't destroy it. The threads will stop you."

"What do you mean?" she demanded. "It's just a book!"

"It's never just a book," he said. "It's a piece of the Caravan, and the threads protect it. If you try to burn it, it'll only come back."

Liora's frustration boiled over, and she turned away, pacing the room. The weight of the situation pressed down on her, suffocating and inescapable. She couldn't stop thinking about the figure in the drawing, the threads that had bound them, the way they had been pulled into the darkness.

"What do we do now?" she asked, her voice breaking.

"We leave," Eryx said. "The longer we stay here, the stronger the pull will get."

Liora nodded, though fear still gnawed at her insides. She

followed Eryx to the door, but as they stepped outside, she felt the faintest tug at her wrist. She glanced back, her eyes landing on the book where it sat on the table.

It was open, its pages glowing faintly in the dim light. And for a moment, she thought she saw the figure in the drawing move, their head tilting as though they were watching her leave.

"Liora," Eryx said sharply, snapping her out of the trance. "Don't look back."

She tore her gaze away, her heart pounding as she followed him into the forest. But the image of the marked book stayed with her, seared into her mind like a brand.

And as they disappeared into the shadows, the faint melody of the Caravan began to play once more, its haunting tune a reminder that the threads were always watching. Always waiting.

Eleven

The Caravan's Curse

The forest was alive with whispers that Liora couldn't escape. Each step she took seemed to echo with faint voices, their murmurs swirling through the air like a haunting breeze. She kept her head down, her fists clenched at her sides, but the sensation of being watched was unshakable. The threads were everywhere now, faint silvery strands that wove through the trees and shimmered faintly in the dying light.

Eryx walked ahead, his strides purposeful but tense. His silence had stretched thin between them since they'd left the abandoned building. Liora wanted to question him, to demand answers about the book, the threads, and the figure she had seen within its pages. But she was afraid of what he might say—or worse, what he might refuse to say.

The Caravan's Curse

When the trees thinned and revealed a narrow path winding through the mist, Eryx finally stopped. He turned to her, his expression grim. "We can't keep going without talking about it," he said.

Liora folded her arms, her pulse quickening. "Talking about what?"

"The book," he said. "What you saw. What it means."

She hesitated, the memory of the figure in the book still vivid in her mind. "You said it wasn't me," she said carefully. "But it felt like it was."

"It wasn't you," he said firmly. "But it could be."

The words hit her like a blow, and she took an involuntary step back. "What are you saying?" she asked, her voice trembling. "That I'm destined to end up like them?"

Eryx's jaw tightened. "Destiny is a strong word," he said. "But the Caravan's curse is powerful. It feeds on people like you."

"People like me?" she repeated, her anger flaring. "What does that even mean?"

"It means you were chosen," he said. "The Caravan doesn't just take anyone. It seeks out those who are lost, those who carry something inside them—grief, guilt, regret. The threads latch onto that and use it to bind you."

Liora's chest tightened, a wave of indignation rising in her. "I didn't ask for this," she said. "I didn't choose to be part of their story."

"None of us did," Eryx said quietly. "But once the threads find you, they don't let go."

The weight of his words settled over her, suffocating and inescapable. She turned away, her eyes scanning the darkened forest. The threads seemed to shimmer more brightly now, their glow pulsing faintly like the rhythm of a heartbeat.

"So what do I do?" she asked finally. "How do I break free?"

Eryx was silent for a long moment, and when he spoke, his voice was heavy with reluctance. "To break free of the Caravan, you have to sever the thread."

"That's it?" she said, turning to face him. "How do we do that?"

"It's not that simple," he said. "The thread isn't just a connection—it's a part of you now. Severing it means severing a piece of yourself."

Liora stared at him, her heart pounding. "What happens if I don't?"

Eryx met her gaze, his expression grave. "Then you'll become part of the Caravan. Forever."

The finality in his tone sent a chill down her spine. She turned away, her thoughts racing. "There has to be another way," she said. "Something less... permanent."

"There isn't," Eryx said. "The Caravan's curse doesn't leave room for negotiation. Either you break the thread, or it binds you completely."

Liora shook her head, refusing to accept his words. "You broke free," she said. "How did you do it?"

Eryx hesitated, his eyes darkening. "It cost me more than you can imagine," he said finally. "And I wouldn't wish that price on anyone."

Before Liora could press him further, a sound cut through the air—a low, mournful wail that sent shivers down her spine. She froze, her eyes darting to Eryx, who had already drawn his sword.

"They're close," he said, his voice low and urgent. "We need to move."

"What is it?" she whispered, gripping her knife tightly.

"The shadows," he said. "They're the Caravan's hunters. They track anyone who resists the threads."

Liora's blood ran cold. "How do we stop them?"

"We don't," he said. "We outrun them."

He grabbed her arm and pulled her down the path, their footsteps pounding against the earth. The wail grew louder, joined by a chorus of otherworldly cries that seemed to echo from every direction. Liora's heart raced as the threads around them began to shift, their glow intensifying as though responding to the sound.

"They're using the threads to track us," she said, her voice breathless.

"Then stop thinking about them," Eryx snapped. "The more you focus on the threads, the stronger their pull will be."

Liora tried to clear her mind, but it was impossible. The threads seemed to pulse with a life of their own, weaving through the air like living things. She could feel their pull, faint but insistent, tugging at her wrist and her thoughts.

The path narrowed as they plunged deeper into the forest, the trees pressing close on either side. The cries of the shadows were deafening now, and Liora felt a chill sweep over her as dark shapes began to materialize in the mist. They were indistinct at first, little more than flickering outlines, but as they drew closer, she could see the twisted forms of their bodies, the way they moved with unnatural grace.

"They're getting closer," she said, panic rising in her voice.

Eryx didn't respond. He turned sharply, leading her off the path and into the dense undergrowth. Branches scratched at her arms and face as they pushed through the foliage, but she didn't dare slow down. The shadows followed, their forms gliding effortlessly through the trees.

"We're not going to outrun them," she said, her voice trembling.

"We don't have to," Eryx said. "We just need to buy time."

"For what?" she demanded.

"For this," he said, pulling her into a small clearing. He turned to face her, his expression fierce. "The threads are tied to the curse, and the curse is tied to the Caravan. If you want to break free, you need to confront it."

"Confront it?" she repeated, her heart pounding. "How?"

"By facing what it's feeding on," he said. "Your fear, your guilt, your regrets. The threads won't let go until you make peace with yourself."

Liora stared at him, her mind reeling. "You're saying this is my fault?" she said, anger bubbling to the surface.

"No," he said firmly. "But the Caravan preys on what's already there. If you don't face it, the curse will consume you."

Before she could respond, the shadows descended, their cries piercing the air like a thousand knives. Eryx raised his sword, his stance defensive as the first shadow lunged at him. Liora gripped her knife, her hands trembling as she prepared to fight.

But even as she raised her weapon, she felt the threads tighten around her wrist, pulling her thoughts inward. The shadows seemed to blur, their forms shifting as her vision began to fade. And in the darkness, she heard the faint, familiar melody of the Caravan, a haunting tune that seemed to call her name.

"Liora!" Eryx's voice cut through the haze, pulling her back. "Focus!"

She blinked, her vision clearing just in time to see a shadow lunging toward her. She dodged to the side, her heart pounding as the creature's claws raked the air where she had been standing. Eryx slashed at another shadow, his movements precise and controlled.

"We can't keep this up," he said, his voice strained. "You need to break the thread. Now."

Liora's breath came in ragged gasps as she clutched her wrist, the thread pulsing faintly beneath her skin. She closed her eyes, trying to block out the chaos around her, and focused on the thread.

The melody of the Caravan grew louder, wrapping around her like a shroud. Images flashed through her mind—memories she had buried, fears she had ignored. She saw herself as a child, lost and alone in the aftermath of a storm. She saw her mother's face, etched with disappointment. She saw the life she had left behind, the choices she had made, the guilt she carried like a weight on her soul.

The Caravan's Curse

And then she saw the thread, a glowing strand that connected her to the shadows, to the Caravan, to everything she feared. It pulsed faintly, its light flickering as though it were alive.

"Cut it," Eryx's voice echoed in her mind. "You have to cut it."

Her fingers tightened around her knife, and she raised it, the blade trembling as she brought it down toward her wrist. The thread pulsed one last time, and then it snapped, its light fading into darkness.

The shadows recoiled, their cries fading as they dissolved into the mist. The forest grew still, and Liora collapsed to her knees, her breath coming in shallow gasps.

Eryx knelt beside her, his expression unreadable. "You did it," he said softly.

Liora looked at her wrist, the faint mark where the thread had been already fading. She felt lighter, freer, but the weight of what she had seen still lingered.

The Caravan's curse was broken, but she knew the fight was far from over. And as the silence of the forest settled around them, she couldn't shake the feeling that the Caravan was still watching, waiting for its next move.

Twelve

A Pact with the Shadows

The forest was eerily silent after the shadows retreated, their presence leaving behind an oppressive stillness that seemed to press against Liora's chest. She sat on the forest floor, her knees drawn to her chest and her back against a gnarled tree. Her wrist no longer bore the faint glow of the thread, but the mark it left within her—a strange emptiness—remained. She stared at the ground, her mind swirling with what she had done.

"You cut the thread," Eryx said, standing a few feet away with his sword still drawn. His tone was measured, but his eyes held a mixture of relief and something else—something heavier, like regret.

Liora didn't answer right away. Her fingers absently traced the bare skin of her wrist, where the thread had once pulsed with life. "It felt like cutting a part of myself," she said finally, her voice barely audible.

Eryx sheathed his sword, stepping closer but keeping a deliberate distance. "That's because it was," he said. "The Caravan doesn't just take people; it takes pieces of them. And when you sever the thread, you lose a piece forever."

Liora looked up at him, her brow furrowing. "You said breaking the thread would free me. But now I feel… hollow."

"That's the price of freedom," he said, his voice low. "It's not a clean break. The Caravan takes something from everyone it touches."

"What did it take from you?" she asked, her gaze narrowing.

Eryx froze, his jaw tightening as he avoided her eyes. The pause was telling, and Liora's heart sank as she realized he had no intention of answering. "It doesn't matter," he said finally. "What matters is that you're free now."

"Am I?" she shot back, her voice rising. "Or did I just trade one kind of control for another?"

Before Eryx could respond, a low, resonant hum rippled through the forest. Liora stiffened, her breath catching in her throat as the sound grew louder, vibrating through the ground beneath her. It was familiar yet alien, a sound that seemed to come from everywhere and nowhere at once.

The Eternal Caravan

"The shadows are back," she whispered, gripping her knife tightly.

"No," Eryx said, his voice tense. "This is something else."

The mist thickened, curling around the trees like ghostly fingers. Shapes began to emerge from the fog—not the amorphous forms of the shadows, but figures draped in cloaks, their faces obscured by deep hoods. They moved with an unnerving grace, their footsteps silent as they closed in around Liora and Eryx.

"What are they?" Liora asked, her voice trembling.

"Not shadows," Eryx said, his hand resting on the hilt of his sword. "But not allies, either."

One of the figures stepped forward, their movements fluid and deliberate. When they spoke, their voice was smooth and layered, as though multiple voices were speaking in unison. "You've severed the thread," they said, addressing Liora directly. "But the connection remains."

Liora rose to her feet, her knife clutched tightly in her hand. "What do you mean?"

The figure tilted their head, their hood shifting just enough to reveal the faint glow of two piercing eyes. "The Caravan is not so easily escaped," they said. "It is part of you now, whether you accept it or not."

"She broke the thread," Eryx said, stepping forward to place himself between Liora and the figure. "That should be enough."

"Breaking the thread severs the surface," the figure said. "But the roots run deep. To truly escape, one must make a choice."

"What kind of choice?" Liora asked, her voice steady despite the fear coursing through her.

"A pact," the figure said simply. "An agreement with the shadows."

Eryx's hand tightened around the hilt of his sword. "No," he said firmly. "We're not making any deals."

The figure's glowing eyes shifted to Eryx, their tone turning colder. "You speak with the arrogance of one who has already made such a deal."

Liora's gaze snapped to Eryx, her breath catching. "What are they talking about?" she demanded.

Eryx didn't respond. His silence was louder than any words could have been, and the weight of it settled over Liora like a crushing force. "You made a pact with them," she said, her voice trembling with a mix of anger and disbelief. "Didn't you?"

"It was a long time ago," Eryx said, his voice tight. "And I didn't have a choice."

"There's always a choice," Liora said, her hands clenching into fists. "What did you do?"

Eryx's gaze dropped, his jaw tightening. "I gave them what they wanted," he said finally. "A piece of myself, in exchange for freedom."

The words hit her like a blow, and for a moment, she couldn't breathe. "What did they take?" she asked, her voice barely audible.

"It doesn't matter," he said. "What matters is that you don't make the same mistake."

The figure stepped closer, their presence almost suffocating. "His mistake freed him," they said. "And it can free you as well."

Liora shook her head, her mind racing. "I'm not making a pact with you," she said. "I'm not giving up another piece of myself."

"Then you will remain tethered," the figure said. "The thread may be severed, but the curse remains. Without the pact, the Caravan will find you again. And next time, you will not escape."

The threat hung in the air, heavy and suffocating. Liora turned to Eryx, her eyes pleading. "What do I do?" she asked. "How do I fight this?"

Eryx hesitated, his expression pained. "You have to resist," he said. "No matter what they promise, no matter what they threaten, you can't let them take anything more."

A Pact with the Shadows

"You speak as though resistance is enough," the figure said. "But you know better, don't you? The Caravan does not allow defiance to go unpunished."

Liora's chest tightened, fear and anger warring within her. She looked at the figure, their glowing eyes watching her intently, and felt the weight of their presence pressing down on her. "What do you want from me?" she asked.

"A choice," the figure said. "Offer us a piece of yourself, and we will sever the connection. Refuse, and the Caravan will claim you fully."

Liora's mind raced, the gravity of the decision threatening to overwhelm her. She glanced at Eryx, but his silence offered no comfort. She was alone in this choice, and the realization hit her with crushing force.

"I won't do it," she said finally, her voice trembling but firm. "I've already lost enough."

The figure was silent for a moment, their head tilting as though considering her response. "So be it," they said. "But know this: the Caravan is patient. And it always collects what it is owed."

Without another word, the figures dissolved into the mist, their forms fading like smoke. The oppressive weight in the air lifted, but Liora's chest still felt heavy, her breath coming in shallow gasps.

Eryx stepped toward her, his expression unreadable. "You

made the right choice," he said.

"Did I?" she asked, her voice shaking. "Because it doesn't feel like it."

"You did," he said firmly. "The price they would've taken isn't worth it."

Liora turned away, her gaze fixed on the mist that swirled through the trees. She wanted to believe him, but the figure's words lingered in her mind, a dark promise that refused to be silenced.

The Caravan was still watching, still waiting. And deep down, she knew her fight was far from over.

Thirteen

The Mirror of Truth

The mist hung low and heavy as Liora and Eryx trudged deeper into the forest. Each step seemed to amplify the oppressive silence around them, broken only by the occasional rustling of leaves or the distant cry of an unseen creature. The shadows between the trees appeared to shift, twisting into shapes that disappeared the moment Liora tried to focus on them. Her chest felt tight, every breath weighed down by the weight of the pact she had refused.

"We need to find shelter," Eryx said finally, his voice breaking the stillness. "The Caravan's influence is stronger at night."

Liora wanted to argue, to tell him that the Caravan's influence never seemed to weaken, day or night. But her exhaustion had robbed her of the energy for words. Instead, she nodded, her eyes scanning the forest for anything resembling safety.

The Eternal Caravan

It was nearly twilight when they stumbled upon the ruin. The structure was ancient, its stone walls cracked and weathered by time. Ivy climbed its surface, and half of its roof had caved in, leaving the interior exposed to the open sky. A large wooden door hung precariously on rusted hinges, creaking faintly as the wind teased it.

"This will do," Eryx said, stepping inside cautiously.

Liora followed, her footsteps echoing on the stone floor. The interior was dimly lit by the fading light of the setting sun, casting long shadows that stretched across the room. The air was cold and damp, carrying the faint scent of earth and decay.

"What is this place?" she asked, her voice hushed.

Eryx shrugged. "A remnant of something older than the Caravan. It doesn't matter. It's abandoned, and it'll keep us hidden for now."

Liora wandered further into the room, her gaze falling on an ornate mirror mounted on the far wall. It was out of place among the ruin, its gilded frame untouched by the decay that surrounded it. The glass was flawless, reflecting the dim light with an almost unnatural clarity.

"Eryx," she called, her voice tinged with unease. "Look at this."

He joined her, his eyes narrowing as he studied the mirror. "That shouldn't be here," he said, his tone sharp.

The Mirror of Truth

"What do you mean?" she asked, stepping closer to it.

"Mirrors like this are tied to the Caravan," he said. "They're not just reflections. They show you things—things you might not want to see."

Liora's stomach churned, but she couldn't look away from the mirror. Something about it drew her in, a magnetic pull that sent a shiver down her spine. "What kind of things?" she asked.

Eryx hesitated, his jaw tightening. "Truths," he said finally. "But not in the way you think. They show you what the Caravan wants you to see."

She frowned, her reflection staring back at her with an unsettling intensity. "Have you looked into one of these before?" she asked.

"Yes," he admitted, his voice low. "And I'll never do it again."

Liora glanced at him, the tension in his posture evident. She wanted to ask what he had seen, but the words caught in her throat. Instead, she turned back to the mirror, her fingers brushing against the cool surface of the glass.

The moment her skin made contact, the room around her seemed to shift. The air grew colder, and the light dimmed until it was barely more than a faint glow. Her reflection in the mirror flickered, distorting and changing until it was no longer her own.

She saw herself standing in a vast field, the sky above her painted in hues of red and gold. The threads she had severed were still wrapped around her wrists, but they glowed with an eerie light, pulsating in time with her heartbeat. She tried to move, but her body felt heavy, as though she were rooted to the ground.

Then the scene shifted. She was no longer alone in the field. Figures emerged from the shadows, their faces obscured by hoods, their movements slow and deliberate. They surrounded her, their hands outstretched as though beckoning her to join them.

"Liora." The voice was soft, almost tender, but it sent a chill down her spine. She turned toward the source, her breath catching in her throat.

It was the masked man from the dance, his glittering mask catching the fading light. He stepped closer, his presence suffocating, and held out a hand. "You cannot run from what you are," he said. "You cannot escape your place in the story."

"I don't want to be part of your story," she said, her voice trembling but firm.

The masked man tilted his head, his expression unreadable behind the mask. "You already are," he said. "The moment you heard the song, the threads began weaving you into the Caravan's tapestry. Severing the thread only delays the inevitable."

"No," she said, shaking her head. "I won't let you take me."

"You have no choice," he said, his tone laced with finality. "The Caravan is eternal, and so is its curse. You cannot escape it. You can only choose how you play your part."

The figures around her moved closer, their hands brushing against her skin. She felt their cold touch, their presence pressing in on her from all sides. Panic surged within her, and she struggled to move, to break free, but the threads tightened, holding her in place.

"Liora!" Eryx's voice cut through the illusion like a blade, pulling her back to reality.

She gasped, stumbling away from the mirror as though it had burned her. The room was as it had been before, the air heavy but still. Eryx was at her side, his hands gripping her shoulders tightly.

"What did you see?" he demanded.

She shook her head, her breath coming in ragged gasps. "They're still there," she said, her voice shaking. "The threads. They're still pulling me in."

Eryx's jaw tightened, and he glanced at the mirror, his expression dark. "That's what they do," he said. "They show you your fears, your doubts, your failures. Anything to make you question yourself."

"It felt real," she said, her hands trembling. "Like I was already part of them."

"You're not," he said firmly. "Not yet."

Liora looked at the mirror again, her reflection once more her own. But she couldn't shake the feeling that something was watching her from the other side, waiting for her to look away.

"We need to destroy it," she said, her voice steady despite the fear in her chest.

"You can't," Eryx said. "The mirror is part of the Caravan. If you try to destroy it, it'll just come back somewhere else."

"Then what do we do?" she asked, her frustration boiling over.

"We leave," he said. "And we don't look back."

Liora hesitated, her eyes lingering on the mirror. She wanted to believe Eryx, to trust that leaving would be enough. But the image of the masked man, the pull of the threads, the suffocating weight of their touch—it all lingered in her mind, a constant reminder that the Caravan was always watching.

As they stepped out of the ruin and into the night, the mirror's faint glow remained visible through the doorway, a silent testament to the truth Liora could no longer ignore.

The Caravan's curse wasn't just a story—it was her reality. And no matter how far she ran, she couldn't escape the threads that bound her to it.

Fourteen

The Caravan Attacked

The night was restless and alive with unease. The forest, which had become their constant companion, now felt suffocating. Every crack of a branch or rustle of leaves set Liora's nerves on edge. Even Eryx, usually composed and calculating, seemed tenser than usual, his hand never straying far from the hilt of his sword.

The threads, though invisible for now, felt like they were everywhere, lingering just beyond sight, waiting to ensnare them again. The faint echo of the Caravan's melody seemed to hum in the distance, growing louder with each step they took.

"We're getting close," Eryx said, his voice low and guarded.

"Close to what?" Liora asked, her exhaustion laced with frustration. "Another trap?"

The Caravan Attacked

Eryx stopped, turning to face her with an intensity that made her stomach twist. "Close to the Caravan," he said. "They're ahead. This is our chance to get answers."

"Answers?" Liora's voice rose, disbelief seeping through her tone. "Do you think they'll just hand over the truth if we ask nicely? Eryx, this is insane."

"Do you have a better plan?" he shot back, his eyes narrowing. "If we don't confront them, the threads will never let you go. Running isn't enough."

She opened her mouth to argue, but the weight of his words silenced her. He was right—every step away from the Caravan felt like dragging an anchor behind her. No matter how far they ran, the threads would always find her.

"Fine," she said finally, her voice steadying. "But if this goes wrong—"

"It won't," he interrupted, though the tension in his voice betrayed his own doubts. "We'll make it work."

The forest thinned as they continued, giving way to a wide, open field bathed in the pale glow of the moon. At its center, the Caravan waited—a collection of ornate wagons and shadowy figures that moved in eerie synchronization. The air was thick with the sound of the melody, haunting and hypnotic, wrapping around them like a veil.

Liora hesitated at the edge of the field, her chest tightening as she took in the sight. The wagons were unlike anything she had expected, their surfaces adorned with intricate carvings that seemed to shift and writhe in the moonlight. The figures moved silently, their hooded forms gliding between the wagons with a grace that sent shivers down her spine.

"We can't just walk in there," she whispered. "They'll see us."

"They already know we're here," Eryx said grimly. "The threads told them."

Liora's stomach dropped, but she forced herself to move forward, her steps hesitant but resolute. Eryx walked beside her, his sword drawn but held low, a quiet promise of readiness. They approached the edge of the Caravan, the air growing colder with each step.

Suddenly, the melody stopped.

The silence was deafening, more oppressive than the music had been. The figures froze, their heads turning in unison toward Liora and Eryx. The absence of movement made the scene feel like a painting, frozen in time and alive with latent menace.

Then, the masked man appeared.

He stepped out from behind one of the wagons, his presence commanding and suffocating. His glittering mask caught the moonlight, and the air seemed to grow heavier with each step he took toward them.

The Caravan Attacked

"You return to us," he said, his voice smooth and echoing, as though it came from everywhere at once. "How predictable."

"We're not here to join you," Eryx said, his tone sharp. "We're here for answers."

The masked man tilted his head, the motion almost playful. "Answers?" he repeated, his voice laced with amusement. "And what makes you believe you are owed such a gift?"

Liora stepped forward, her fear giving way to anger. "Because you've already taken enough from me," she said. "You owe me that much."

The masked man chuckled, the sound chilling in its sincerity. "You misunderstand, child," he said. "The Caravan takes only what is offered. You bound yourself to us the moment you listened."

"I didn't have a choice," she shot back.

"There is always a choice," the man said. "You simply chose not to hear it."

Before Liora could respond, the air around them shifted. A low, rumbling growl echoed across the field, and the figures of the Caravan tensed, their heads snapping toward the forest. Eryx's hand went to his sword, his body going rigid as he scanned the darkness.

"What is that?" Liora whispered.

The Eternal Caravan

"Not shadows," Eryx said, his voice grim. "Something else."

The growl came again, louder this time, accompanied by the sound of snapping branches. The figures of the Caravan began to move, their eerie synchronization giving way to something frantic, almost panicked.

"Protect the Caravan," the masked man commanded, his voice losing its calm veneer. "Do not let them breach."

Liora's heart pounded as she watched the figures spring into action, their movements unnaturally fast and precise. The air grew colder, and the faint glow of the threads appeared, weaving through the field like living things.

"Eryx," she said, her voice shaking. "What's happening?"

"They're under attack," he said, his tone tinged with disbelief. "Something's coming for them."

The forest erupted with movement, and Liora's breath caught in her throat as massive shapes burst from the treeline. They were beasts, their forms shadowy and indistinct, but their presence was undeniable. Their glowing eyes burned like embers, and their growls rumbled through the air like thunder.

The beasts charged into the Caravan, their claws slashing through wagons and figures alike. The melody returned, loud and dissonant, as though the Caravan itself were screaming in pain. Liora watched in horror as the figures fought back, their movements swift and deadly but no match for the ferocity of

The Caravan Attacked

the beasts.

"Run," Eryx said, grabbing her arm and pulling her toward the edge of the field.

"But—" she began, her voice drowned out by the chaos around them.

"We can't help them," he said firmly. "This isn't our fight."

They darted toward the treeline, the sounds of battle ringing in their ears. Liora's heart pounded as she glanced back, the sight of the Caravan in ruins seared into her mind. The wagons burned, their ornate carvings consumed by flames, and the figures that had seemed so invincible now lay broken and scattered.

As they reached the safety of the trees, Liora turned to Eryx, her chest heaving. "What was that?" she demanded. "What were those things?"

"I don't know," he said, his voice grim. "But whatever they were, they weren't here for us."

She looked back at the burning Caravan, the flames casting an eerie glow over the field. The masked man was still standing, his presence unwavering despite the destruction around him. He turned toward the forest, his glittering mask catching the firelight, and Liora felt a chill run down her spine.

"He's watching us," she said, her voice barely audible.

"Let him watch," Eryx said. "He has bigger problems now."

They disappeared into the shadows of the forest, the sounds of the battle fading behind them. But as they moved further from the field, Liora couldn't shake the feeling that the Caravan's destruction was only the beginning.

Whatever had attacked them wasn't just a threat to the Caravan—it was a threat to everything. And as the distant echo of the melody reached her ears once more, she knew their fight was far from over.

Fifteen

The Stolen Map

The forest was darker than it had ever been. The usual pale glow of the threads was absent, replaced by an oppressive blackness that seemed to absorb what little moonlight filtered through the canopy. Liora's legs felt heavy as she followed Eryx through the twisted undergrowth, her breath coming in short, shallow bursts. The chaos of the Caravan's attack was still fresh in her mind—the eerie melody, the monstrous beasts, and the masked man's unflinching gaze as the flames consumed everything around him.

"We need to keep moving," Eryx said, his voice low and urgent. He glanced back at her, his face a mask of determination. "If they're tracking us, we don't have much time."

Liora nodded, though her exhaustion was beginning to outweigh her fear. "Do you think the attack was meant for us?"

she asked, her voice barely above a whisper.

Eryx shook his head. "No," he said. "The Caravan has enemies, too. Whatever attacked them, it was after something else."

"Something else," Liora repeated, her mind racing. "Like what?"

He didn't answer immediately, his jaw tightening as though weighing his words. Finally, he said, "Power. Influence. Control. The Caravan holds more than just people—it holds secrets. And secrets are worth killing for."

Liora's stomach twisted. She wanted to press him for more, but the tension in his voice made her hesitate. She turned her attention to the path ahead, her thoughts churning with unanswered questions.

They walked in silence for what felt like hours, the oppressive darkness making it impossible to gauge the passage of time. Liora's muscles ached, and her mind felt foggy, but she forced herself to keep up with Eryx's relentless pace.

Finally, they emerged into a small clearing, the faint light of the moon casting long shadows across the ground. Eryx stopped, his eyes scanning their surroundings before gesturing for Liora to sit. "We'll rest here," he said. "But not for long."

Liora sank onto a fallen log, her body sagging with relief. She watched as Eryx dropped his satchel onto the ground and began rummaging through it, his movements quick and deliberate. He pulled out the blank map, unrolling it carefully and laying it flat on the ground.

"What are you doing?" she asked, her curiosity piqued despite her exhaustion.

"Checking for changes," he said, his gaze fixed on the map. "After what happened back there, it's possible the map—"

He stopped abruptly, his eyes narrowing. Liora leaned forward, her pulse quickening as she followed his gaze. The map, which had been blank since the moment they found it, now bore faint markings. Thin, glowing lines crisscrossed its surface, forming a complex web of paths and symbols that pulsed faintly in the moonlight.

"What does it mean?" she asked, her voice hushed.

"It's a trail," Eryx said, his tone laced with urgency. "A way to the heart of the Caravan."

Liora's chest tightened. "The heart? You mean where it all started?"

"Yes," he said. "And maybe where it can be ended."

Before Liora could respond, a sharp sound cut through the air—a snap, like a branch breaking underfoot. She froze, her eyes darting to the edge of the clearing. Eryx was on his feet in an instant, his sword drawn as he scanned the darkness.

"We're not alone," he said, his voice low.

The silence that followed was deafening, broken only by the faint rustle of leaves. Liora's heart pounded as she gripped her knife, her knuckles white. The shadows seemed to move, shifting and twisting as though alive.

Then, without warning, a figure burst from the treeline, their movements quick and deliberate. They darted toward the map, their hand outstretched, and before Eryx could react, they snatched it from the ground.

"Stop!" Eryx shouted, lunging toward the thief.

The figure was fast, ducking under Eryx's swing and rolling to the side. Liora caught a glimpse of their face—a young man with sharp features and dark eyes that gleamed with determination—before he disappeared into the shadows.

"Liora, stay here!" Eryx commanded, his tone leaving no room for argument as he took off after the thief.

Liora hesitated, her instincts screaming for her to follow. But the darkness around her was suffocating, and the thought of being alone in it made her chest tighten. She gripped her knife tightly, her eyes scanning the clearing for any sign of movement.

Minutes stretched into what felt like hours, the silence amplifying her fear. Then she heard it—a muffled grunt, followed by the clang of metal against metal. She rose to her feet, her heart pounding as she moved toward the sound.

The Stolen Map

The fight came into view as she pushed through the undergrowth. Eryx and the thief were locked in a vicious struggle, their movements quick and brutal. The map lay on the ground between them, its glowing lines casting an eerie light on their faces.

Eryx swung his sword, but the thief was fast, ducking under the blade and delivering a sharp kick to Eryx's side. He stumbled but recovered quickly, his eyes blazing with determination as he pressed the attack.

Liora's gaze shifted to the map. It was unguarded, lying just a few feet away. She didn't think—she acted, darting forward and snatching it up before either man could stop her.

"Liora, run!" Eryx shouted, his voice raw with urgency.

She didn't need to be told twice. She turned and bolted into the forest, the map clutched tightly to her chest. The glow of its markings illuminated her path, guiding her through the darkness as the sounds of the fight faded behind her.

Her lungs burned, and her legs ached, but she didn't stop. She could hear footsteps behind her, growing louder with each passing second. She risked a glance over her shoulder and saw the thief pursuing her, his dark eyes locked onto the map in her hands.

"Give it to me!" he shouted, his voice sharp with desperation.

"Stay back!" she yelled, her voice trembling but defiant.

The Eternal Caravan

The thief was faster, closing the distance between them with alarming speed. Liora's mind raced as she scanned her surroundings, searching for anything she could use to slow him down. Her eyes landed on a dense thicket of brambles up ahead, their sharp thorns glinting faintly in the light of the map.

She veered toward the thicket, plunging into it without hesitation. The thorns tore at her clothes and skin, but she didn't slow down. The thief hesitated at the edge, cursing under his breath before following her.

The thicket gave way to a small clearing, and Liora stumbled to a halt, her chest heaving. The thief emerged moments later, his face twisted with frustration. He didn't speak, his gaze fixed on the map in her hands.

"You don't understand," he said, his voice low and urgent. "That map doesn't belong to you."

"It doesn't belong to you, either," Liora shot back, her grip on the map tightening. "Why do you want it?"

The thief hesitated, his eyes narrowing. "Because it's the only way to stop them," he said. "The Caravan. It's a weapon, and if you don't use it, they will."

His words sent a chill down her spine, but before she could respond, Eryx appeared behind the thief, his sword at the ready. "Step away from her," he said, his voice cold.

The thief froze, his hands raised in surrender. "You don't know

The Stolen Map

what you're dealing with," he said, his tone desperate. "The map isn't what you think it is."

Eryx didn't waver. "We'll decide that," he said. "Now leave."

The thief hesitated for a moment longer before backing away, his eyes lingering on Liora. "You've made a mistake," he said. "And when it's too late, you'll wish you'd listened."

He disappeared into the shadows, his warning hanging heavy in the air. Liora turned to Eryx, her hands trembling as she held out the map. "What do we do now?" she asked.

Eryx took the map, his expression grim. "We keep moving," he said. "And we don't let it out of our sight again."

As they left the clearing, Liora couldn't shake the thief's words. The map was more than just a guide—it was a weapon. And now, it was in their hands.

Sixteen

The Maze of Shadows

The forest thickened as Liora and Eryx pressed onward, the trees standing like silent sentinels in the oppressive darkness. The map's faint glow was their only source of light, its intricate lines and shifting symbols casting eerie patterns on their faces. It was unnerving how alive the map seemed, its markings pulsating like veins filled with liquid light. Liora held her breath each time Eryx traced its paths, as if the map itself might recoil or react to his touch.

"We're here," Eryx said after a long silence, his voice barely audible.

Liora glanced up, her heart sinking at the sight before them. The trees gave way to a towering wall of black stone, jagged and uneven, stretching as far as the eye could see in both directions. It seemed to absorb the faint light of the map, making it appear darker than the surrounding forest. The air here was colder, heavier, as though the stone itself exhaled despair.

"What is this?" she asked, her voice trembling.

Eryx's jaw tightened. "The Maze of Shadows," he said. "It's a barrier the Caravan created to protect its heart. If we're going to get to the source, we have to go through it."

Liora stared at the wall, unease curling in her stomach. "Through it? How? There's no door."

"There's always a way in," Eryx said. "But it won't be easy."

He held up the map, its glow intensifying as he brought it closer to the wall. The lines and symbols shifted, rearranging themselves until a new path emerged, one that pointed directly into the stone.

Liora's pulse quickened. "That doesn't look like a door," she said.

"It isn't," Eryx replied. "The Maze doesn't have doors. It's built to confuse and trap anyone who tries to enter. The map will guide us, but we have to trust it."

"Trust it?" Liora repeated, her voice rising. "The same map that almost got stolen by someone who claimed it's a weapon? That map?"

Eryx turned to her, his expression hard. "If you have a better idea, now's the time to say it."

She opened her mouth to argue but stopped. He was right—there was no other way. With a resigned nod, she stepped closer to the wall, the cold radiating from the stone making her shiver.

Eryx placed his hand on the wall, the map in his other hand glowing brighter. The stone began to shift, its jagged surface rippling like liquid. A narrow opening appeared, just wide enough for them to pass through.

"Stay close to me," Eryx said, his tone firm. "The Maze is alive. If we lose sight of each other, it will separate us."

Liora swallowed hard, her grip tightening on her knife. "Great," she muttered. "Another sentient death trap."

They stepped into the opening, the stone closing behind them with a low, grinding sound. The air inside was colder, the darkness so thick it felt tangible. The map's glow illuminated only a few feet ahead, the shifting lines forming a path that twisted and turned unpredictably.

The silence was suffocating, broken only by the sound of their footsteps echoing on the stone floor. Liora stayed close to Eryx, her eyes darting to every shadow that seemed to stretch and move as they passed. The walls loomed high above them, their surfaces etched with strange markings that pulsed faintly, like the veins of some living creature.

The Maze of Shadows

"How does this thing work?" she asked, nodding toward the map. "How does it know where to go?"

"It's tied to the threads," Eryx said without looking at her. "The Maze and the Caravan are connected. The map draws its guidance from that connection."

"So we're following something tied to the thing we're trying to escape," Liora said, her voice heavy with sarcasm. "Brilliant."

Eryx shot her a warning look but said nothing. They continued in silence, the map's path leading them deeper into the Maze. The air grew heavier with each step, the walls seeming to close in around them. Liora's chest tightened, her breaths coming faster as a sense of unease settled over her.

Then she heard it—a faint whisper, barely audible but unmistakable. It came from the shadows, a soft, insistent murmur that made her skin crawl.

"Do you hear that?" she asked, her voice barely above a whisper.

Eryx nodded, his grip tightening on his sword. "Ignore it," he said. "The Maze feeds on doubt and fear. If you listen to it, it will lead you astray."

Liora tried to focus on the map's glow, but the whispers grew louder, their words slipping into her mind like poison.

"You don't belong here."
  "Turn back while you still can."

"You'll never make it."

She clenched her fists, her nails digging into her palms as she fought to block out the voices. But they didn't stop. They grew louder, more insistent, until it felt like they were coming from inside her own head.

"Eryx," she said, her voice shaking. "It's getting worse."

"Stay focused," he said sharply. "Look at the map. Don't let the Maze distract you."

She forced herself to obey, her eyes locking onto the glowing lines of the map. But the whispers didn't fade. Instead, they changed, their tone shifting from threatening to familiar.

"You can't run forever, Liora."
  "You're already one of them."
  "Come home."

Her steps faltered, her breath catching in her throat. "That voice," she said, her eyes wide. "It's mine."

Eryx stopped, turning to her with a look of alarm. "Don't listen to it," he said. "It's not real."

But it felt real. It sounded real. And as the whispers continued, the shadows around her began to shift, forming shapes that were painfully familiar. She saw herself, standing in the Caravan's field, the threads wrapped tightly around her wrists. She saw her mother, her face etched with disappointment. She saw the life she had left behind, the choices she had made, the regrets that still haunted her.

"Liora!" Eryx's voice snapped her out of the trance. He grabbed her arm, his grip firm but grounding. "Stay with me."

"I can't do this," she said, her voice trembling. "It's too much."

"Yes, you can," he said, his eyes locking onto hers. "The Maze wants you to give up. Don't let it win."

She nodded, her resolve hardening as she focused on the map once more. The path twisted sharply, leading them into a narrow corridor that seemed to stretch endlessly. The whispers faded, but the sense of unease remained, like a shadow that refused to leave.

As they turned another corner, the map's glow dimmed suddenly, the lines flickering as though struggling to stay lit.

"What's happening?" Liora asked, panic creeping into her voice.

"The Maze is trying to sever the connection," Eryx said, his tone grim. "We have to move faster."

They quickened their pace, the flickering light of the map casting unsettling shadows on the walls. The corridor narrowed further, forcing them to walk single file. The air grew colder, each breath forming clouds of mist that hung in the stillness.

Finally, the map's glow steadied, its lines pointing toward a small, circular chamber at the end of the corridor. They stepped inside cautiously, the walls of the chamber covered in intricate carvings that seemed to pulse faintly with light.

At the center of the chamber stood a pedestal, and on it rested a small, ornate key. Its surface was etched with the same shifting markings as the map, and it radiated a faint, otherworldly glow.

"What is that?" Liora asked, her voice barely audible.

"The key to the heart of the Maze," Eryx said. "But taking it won't be easy."

Before she could ask what he meant, the whispers returned, louder and more menacing than before. The shadows in the chamber began to move, detaching themselves from the walls and converging on the pedestal.

Eryx drew his sword, his stance defensive. "Stay close," he said. "This is what the Maze has been waiting for."

Liora gripped her knife, her heart pounding as the shadows closed in. The Maze was alive, and it wasn't going to let them leave without a fight.

Seventeen

A Heart Divided

The forest seemed to close in around them, its oppressive silence broken only by the soft crunch of leaves underfoot. The faint glow of the key in Liora's hand cast ghostly shadows that twisted and writhed on the trees as they moved. The Maze was behind them now, its looming walls swallowed by the distance, but Liora could still feel its presence—an invisible weight that pressed against her chest, reminding her that the danger was far from over.

Eryx walked ahead, his posture tense and his hand resting on the hilt of his sword. The tension between them was palpable, unspoken but unavoidable. Liora had questions—about the key, about the Caravan, about the choices that had led them here—but the words wouldn't come. She didn't know if she wanted answers or if she was afraid of what they might reveal.

"Do you feel that?" she asked finally, breaking the silence.

Eryx glanced back at her, his expression grim. "Feel what?"

"Like the forest is... watching us," she said, her voice barely above a whisper.

He nodded, his gaze scanning the shadows. "That's because it is," he said. "The Caravan's influence doesn't stop at the Maze. The threads reach everywhere."

The mention of the threads sent a shiver down her spine. She glanced at her wrist, half-expecting to see the faint glow of the tether she had severed, but her skin remained unmarked. Still, the memory of its presence lingered, a constant reminder that she was never truly free.

They walked in silence for what felt like hours, the forest growing darker with each passing step. The key's glow was their only source of light, its shifting patterns reflecting off Eryx's blade and the damp, moss-covered ground. Liora couldn't shake the feeling that they were being followed, but every time she turned to look, the forest was empty.

Finally, they reached a clearing. At its center stood an ancient stone altar, its surface cracked and weathered by time. Surrounding it were eight towering statues, each one depicting a figure shrouded in cloaks and veils, their faces obscured. The statues loomed over the altar like silent guardians, their presence both awe-inspiring and unnerving.

A Heart Divided

"What is this place?" Liora asked, her voice trembling.

Eryx approached the altar cautiously, his eyes scanning the statues. "It's a waypoint," he said. "A place where the threads converge. The Caravan uses these to mark its territory, to reinforce its presence."

"Reinforce its presence?" Liora repeated, her stomach twisting. "What does that mean?"

"It means the Caravan's influence is strongest here," he said. "This is where it can reach you the easiest."

Liora's heart pounded as she stepped closer to the altar, her eyes drawn to the strange symbols carved into its surface. They were similar to the markings on the key, shifting and writhing as though alive. She reached out to touch one, but Eryx's hand shot out, grabbing her wrist.

"Don't," he said sharply. "The altar is tied to the threads. Touching it could reconnect you."

She pulled her hand back, her chest tightening. "Then why are we here?"

"Because this is the next step," Eryx said, pulling the map from his satchel. He unrolled it carefully, laying it on the altar. The glow of the key intensified as he held it over the map, the lines and symbols shifting and rearranging themselves.

The map's markings coalesced into a single path, leading

toward a point at the center of the forest. Around it, the lines pulsed faintly, forming a shape that resembled a beating heart.

"The heart of the Caravan," Eryx said, his voice heavy with gravity. "This is where we'll find it."

Liora stared at the map, her mind racing. "And what happens when we get there?" she asked. "Do we destroy it? Bargain with it? What's the plan?"

Eryx's jaw tightened, and he avoided her gaze. "We'll figure it out when we get there," he said.

"That's not good enough," she snapped, her fear and frustration boiling over. "You brought me this far, Eryx. You owe me more than vague promises and half-truths."

He turned to her, his eyes hard. "You think I have all the answers?" he asked, his voice low and sharp. "I've been running from the Caravan my whole life, Liora. Everything I've done, every choice I've made, has been to survive. I don't know what we'll find at the heart, but I know this is our only chance to stop it."

His words hung in the air, heavy with unspoken pain. Liora stared at him, her anger faltering. She wanted to believe him, to trust that he was doing his best, but the uncertainty in his voice sent a chill through her.

Before she could respond, a sound cut through the silence—a low, mournful wail that sent shivers down her spine. It echoed through the clearing, growing louder and more insistent.

"They're here," Eryx said, his voice tense. He grabbed the key and the map, stuffing them into his satchel. "We need to move."

"What is it?" Liora asked, her pulse racing.

"Hunters," he said, his hand going to his sword. "The Caravan's enforcers. They track anyone who gets too close to the heart."

The wail grew louder, accompanied by the sound of rustling leaves and snapping branches. Liora's breath quickened as shadows began to emerge from the forest, their forms indistinct but unmistakably menacing.

"Run," Eryx said, drawing his sword. "I'll hold them off."

"No," she said, her voice shaking but firm. "We're in this together."

He hesitated, his eyes searching hers, and then he nodded. "Stay close," he said. "And don't stop moving."

They darted into the forest, the shadows close behind. The hunters moved with unnatural speed, their forms flickering and shifting as they pursued. Liora's lungs burned as she ran, her legs aching with the effort, but she didn't dare slow down.

The key's glow lit their path, guiding them through the dense undergrowth. The forest seemed to twist and shift around them, the trees bending and warping as if alive. Liora could feel the hunters closing in, their presence a cold, suffocating weight.

"Eryx!" she shouted, her voice filled with panic. "We're not going to make it!"

"We will," he said, though his voice was strained. "Just keep going."

The key's light flared suddenly, and the path ahead opened into another clearing. At its center stood a massive, ancient tree, its gnarled branches reaching toward the sky. The heart of the Caravan.

Liora skidded to a stop, her breath coming in ragged gasps. The tree pulsed with a faint, rhythmic light, its bark etched with the same shifting symbols as the map and the key. The hunters halted at the edge of the clearing, their forms writhing as if unable to cross.

"We're here," Eryx said, his voice filled with both awe and dread.

Liora stared at the tree, her chest tightening with a mix of fear and determination. "Now what?" she asked.

Eryx's grip on his sword tightened, his eyes locked on the tree. "Now we end this."

The heart of the Caravan awaited them, its power radiating through the clearing like a heartbeat. And as Liora stepped forward, the key in her hand glowing brighter than ever, she knew their choices here would decide everything.

Eighteen

The Caravan Fractures

The Caravan Fractures

The air in the heart of the forest was charged with an energy so thick it felt like walking through a storm. The glow of the ancient key in Liora's hand pulsed in rhythm with the ominous melody that filled the air. Every step closer to the massive tree—the Caravan's heart—made the threads weaving through the clearing more erratic, like a spider's web trembling under the weight of something massive and unseen.

Eryx walked beside her, his sword drawn, his posture tense. He was ready to fight, but deep down, he knew that brute strength wouldn't be enough. The Caravan was too vast, too deeply rooted in the fabric of their world. Still, he couldn't let Liora face this alone. Not when he had seen how the threads had started to claim her, shimmering faintly on her wrists like ghostly shackles.

"Are you ready?" he asked, his voice low.

"I don't know if anyone could ever be ready for this," Liora replied, her gaze fixed on the glowing symbols etched into the tree's gnarled trunk. "But I'm here. And I'm not leaving."

The tree seemed alive, its roots shifting ever so slightly, its massive branches creaking as if adjusting to their presence. The carvings on its bark glowed faintly, illuminating the threads that emanated from its base and stretched outward into the forest like veins. It was both beautiful and terrifying—a living representation of the Caravan's power.

As they approached, the ground beneath their feet began to tremble, a low, rhythmic pulse that matched the melody echoing through the air. The threads surrounding the tree flickered, their glow dimming and intensifying erratically.

"Something's wrong," Eryx said, his voice tinged with unease. "The threads... they're unstable."

Liora nodded, gripping the key tighter. She could feel it too—a tension in the air, as if the threads were on the verge of snapping. The tree's glow faltered, and the melody shifted, its harmonious rhythm fracturing into dissonant, jarring notes.

Then the first thread broke.

The sound was deafening, a high-pitched crack that echoed through the clearing. The thread snapped like a whip, its glowing light dissipating into the air. Liora stumbled back, her heart racing as the tree shuddered violently.

"What's happening?" she shouted, panic rising in her voice.

"The Caravan is unraveling," Eryx said, his eyes wide with alarm. "The threads can't hold it together anymore."

The ground beneath them split open, jagged cracks spreading outward from the tree's base. More threads snapped, their light scattering like embers in the wind. The air grew colder, heavier, as if the world itself was holding its breath.

And then the hunters arrived.

They emerged from the shadows, their forms flickering and shifting like living silhouettes. Their hollow eyes glowed faintly, and their movements were unnaturally smooth, almost liquid. There were more of them than Liora had ever seen, dozens upon dozens, each one radiating the same cold, unrelenting menace.

"They're here to protect the Caravan," Eryx said, raising his sword. "But if the threads are breaking—"

"They'll think we're the cause," Liora finished, her voice trembling.

The hunters didn't wait for an explanation. They moved as one, surging toward Liora and Eryx with deadly precision. Eryx stepped forward, his sword flashing as he intercepted the first wave. His movements were swift and calculated, but for every hunter he cut down, two more took its place.

"Liora, stay back!" he shouted, his voice strained. "I'll hold them off!"

"I can't just stand here!" she yelled, gripping the key. Its glow flared as if responding to her emotions, the intricate symbols on its surface shifting and writhing. She didn't know how to use it, but she could feel its power—wild and untamed, waiting for her command.

A hunter lunged at her, its claws slicing through the air. Liora raised the key instinctively, and a burst of light erupted from its surface, engulfing the hunter in a searing glow. The creature dissolved, its form disintegrating like ash in the wind.

Eryx glanced back, his expression a mix of relief and shock. "How did you do that?"

"I don't know!" she admitted, her voice shaking. "But I think the key—"

Before she could finish, the ground beneath the tree gave way, collapsing into a massive crater. The tree shuddered, its branches thrashing wildly as more threads snapped, their light scattering like shooting stars. The melody fractured further, its once-hypnotic rhythm devolving into a chaotic cacophony.

And then she heard it—the voice.

It was deep and resonant, echoing from the very heart of the tree. **"Who dares disrupt the weave?"**

Liora froze, her chest tightening as the voice reverberated through her. It wasn't like the whispers she had heard before; this was something far older, far more powerful.

"We're not here to disrupt anything," she said, her voice trembling but firm. "We're here to stop the Caravan from taking any more lives."

The voice laughed, a low, rumbling sound that sent shivers

down her spine. **"The Caravan does not take. It weaves. It connects. You misunderstand its purpose."**

"It's not connection," Eryx snapped, his sword cutting through another hunter. "It's control. You trap people in your threads and force them to be part of your story."

"All stories require sacrifice," the voice said. **"Without the threads, there is no balance. No order."**

"Then maybe it's time for a new story," Liora said, stepping forward. The key in her hand glowed brighter, its light casting long shadows across the clearing. "One where people get to choose their own paths."

The tree shuddered violently, its branches thrashing as if in pain. **"You cannot rewrite what has been woven. To sever the threads is to destroy the weave. Are you prepared for the consequences?"**

Liora hesitated, the weight of the decision pressing down on her. She glanced at Eryx, his face etched with determination despite the chaos around them. She thought of the lives the Caravan had claimed, the people who had been bound to its cursed threads. And she thought of the stories yet to be written, the choices yet to be made.

"Yes," she said, her voice steady. "I'm prepared."

The key flared, its light consuming the clearing. The hunters froze, their forms dissolving into the air as the threads around them unraveled. The tree let out a deep, guttural groan, its bark splintering and cracking as the glow of its carvings faded.

"Liora!" Eryx shouted, reaching for her as the ground beneath her feet began to crumble.

The threads coiled around her, their light pulsing erratically as if fighting to maintain their hold. She felt their pull, their desperate attempt to bind her to the Caravan's story. But she refused to let them win.

With a surge of determination, she thrust the key into the tree's trunk. The moment the metal touched the wood, a blinding light erupted, engulfing everything in its path. The threads snapped in unison, their light extinguished as the tree collapsed into the crater.

When the light faded, the clearing was silent. The tree was gone, reduced to a smoldering heap of ash and embers. The threads had vanished, their presence erased from the air. The melody of the Caravan was no more.

Liora stood at the edge of the crater, her chest heaving as she clutched the key. She turned to Eryx, her eyes filled with exhaustion and determination. "It's over," she said, her voice barely above a whisper.

Eryx nodded, his expression a mix of relief and sorrow. "For now," he said. "But the Caravan's story isn't finished yet."

And deep in the shadows of the forest, something watched, waiting for its chance to weave a new thread.

Nineteen

The Eternal Sacrifice

The ancient tree loomed over them, its gnarled roots stretching out like skeletal fingers, its twisted branches clawing at the sky. The faint, rhythmic pulse emanating from the trunk filled the clearing with a sense of foreboding, as if the very heart of the forest were beating in time with some unseen force. The air was heavy, oppressive, each breath feeling like a struggle.

Liora stood at the edge of the clearing, the glowing key clutched tightly in her hand. The light it emitted was stronger now, its pulsing rhythm syncing with that of the tree. The connection was undeniable, a tether linking the two together in a way that felt both powerful and terrifying.

Eryx stood beside her, his sword drawn and his eyes scanning their surroundings. The hunters had stopped at the edge of the clearing, their shadowy forms writhing as though held back by an invisible barrier. Their low, guttural growls echoed in the stillness, a constant reminder of the danger lurking just beyond reach.

"This is it," Eryx said, his voice low and steady. "The heart of the Caravan."

Liora swallowed hard, her gaze fixed on the tree. "It doesn't look like a heart," she said, her voice trembling. "It looks like a prison."

"In a way, it is," Eryx replied. "The Caravan's power is tied to this place. Everything it does, every thread it weaves, comes from here."

"So if we destroy it…" Liora began, her words trailing off as the weight of the task settled over her.

"We destroy the Caravan," Eryx finished. "And everything it's connected to."

Liora's stomach twisted. The key in her hand felt heavier now, its glow almost blinding. She could feel the weight of its power, the responsibility it carried. But she could also feel something else—something dark and insidious, a whispering voice that seemed to come from the tree itself.

"You cannot destroy what you do not understand."

The voice was soft, almost soothing, but it sent a chill down her spine. She glanced at Eryx, but his expression told her he hadn't heard it. The voice was meant for her alone.

"Did you hear that?" she asked, her voice barely audible.

"Hear what?" Eryx replied, his eyes narrowing.

"Nothing," she said quickly, shaking her head. "It's nothing."

But it wasn't nothing. The voice was still there, a faint whisper at the edge of her consciousness. It seemed to echo from the tree itself, its tone shifting from soothing to commanding.

"You cannot sever the threads without consequence."

Liora took a step forward, her breath catching as the ground beneath her feet seemed to pulse in time with the tree. The key in her hand grew warmer, its glow intensifying until it felt like it was burning her skin.

"Liora, stop," Eryx said, his voice sharp. "You don't know what you're dealing with."

"I have to do this," she said, her voice shaking. "If we don't end this now, the Caravan will never stop."

Eryx moved to block her path, his expression hard. "There's a reason no one's done this before," he said. "The Caravan's power isn't just tied to the tree. It's tied to us. To everyone who's ever been marked. Destroying it could destroy everything."

The Eternal Sacrifice

"Then what's the alternative?" Liora demanded, her frustration boiling over. "Letting it continue? Letting it take more people, more lives?"

Eryx's jaw tightened, but he didn't answer. His silence spoke volumes.

Liora stepped past him, her resolve hardening. She approached the tree, the whispers growing louder with each step. The bark seemed to shift and writhe, the symbols etched into its surface glowing faintly in response to the key.

As she reached the base of the tree, the whispers coalesced into a single voice, deep and resonant. "To end the Caravan, you must become it."

"What does that mean?" Liora asked aloud, her voice trembling. "I don't want to be part of this."

"The Caravan cannot exist without a weaver," the voice replied. "To sever the threads, you must take their place."

She froze, the weight of the words sinking in. "You're saying I have to... take on the Caravan's power?"

"You hold the key," the voice said. "The choice is yours. But know this: without a weaver, the threads will unravel. And with them, all who are bound to the Caravan."

Liora's breath caught in her throat. She turned to Eryx, her voice shaking. "Is that true? If I destroy this... does it kill everyone the Caravan's connected to?"

Eryx's expression darkened, and he looked away. "It's possible," he admitted. "The Caravan's threads are tied to its heart. Severing them could unravel everything."

She stared at him, her heart pounding. "You knew this," she said, her voice rising. "You knew this and you didn't tell me?"

"I didn't know for sure," he said. "And if I had told you, would it have changed anything?"

Liora didn't answer. Her mind was racing, the weight of the decision crushing her. The key pulsed in her hand, its glow now almost unbearable.

"What happens if I take the Caravan's place?" she asked, her voice barely audible.

Eryx hesitated, his gaze meeting hers. "You'd become its weaver," he said. "Its heart. You'd control the threads, but you'd be bound to them. Forever."

The word hung in the air, heavy and suffocating. Liora turned back to the tree, the whispers now a cacophony of voices, each one urging her to make a choice.

She closed her eyes, taking a deep, steadying breath. She thought of the people the Caravan had taken, the lives it had consumed. She thought of the hunters, the shadows, the endless pursuit that had brought her here.

And then she thought of Eryx. Of his sacrifices. Of the way he had fought to help her, even when he had every reason to give up.

"I can't let this continue," she said, her voice steady despite the fear in her chest.

"Liora, wait—" Eryx began, but she didn't let him finish.

She raised the key, its light blazing as she pressed it against the tree's surface. The moment the metal touched the bark, a surge of energy shot through her, blinding and overwhelming. The whispers turned to screams, the symbols on the tree flaring to life as the ground beneath her feet shook violently.

The tree began to crack and splinter, its light pouring out in blinding rays. Liora felt the threads reaching for her, wrapping around her wrists, her arms, her very soul. The pain was excruciating, but she didn't let go.

"Liora!" Eryx shouted, his voice breaking through the chaos. "Don't do this!"

She turned to him, her vision blurred by tears and light. "It's the only way," she said, her voice trembling. "I have to stop it."

The tree shuddered, its light dimming as the threads tightened around her. The last thing she saw was Eryx reaching for her, his face etched with desperation, before the light consumed her completely.

When the light faded, the clearing was silent. The tree was gone, its roots and branches reduced to ash. The hunters at the edge of the clearing had vanished, their forms dissipated like smoke.

Eryx stood alone, his sword falling from his hand as he stared at the spot where Liora had been. The key lay on the ground, its glow extinguished.

And in the distance, the faint melody of the Caravan began to play once more, a haunting reminder that the story was far from over.

Twenty

The Last Dance

The melody was faint at first, a ghost of a sound carried on the wind. It was haunting and familiar, weaving its way through the trees with an almost tangible weight. Eryx stood frozen in the clearing, his sword limp in his hand as he stared at the scorched earth where the ancient tree had stood. The ash swirled in the faint breeze, settling into the lines of his weathered face. The glow of the key had faded, but its presence was still palpable—a quiet hum that resonated in his chest.

He had failed.

The thought echoed in his mind, sharp and unrelenting. He had promised to protect Liora, to guide her, to ensure she wouldn't fall victim to the Caravan's curse. And yet, she was gone, consumed by the very power they had sought to destroy.

The threads had taken her, wrapping around her in a final, unyielding embrace.

The melody grew louder, cutting through the oppressive silence. Eryx gritted his teeth, the sound scraping against his nerves like jagged glass. It was the same melody that had haunted his dreams for years, the same song that had marked the beginning of his own descent into the Caravan's grasp.

"Liora," he whispered, his voice barely audible.

The clearing around him began to shift, the air growing colder and heavier. The shadows lengthened, stretching unnaturally as they twisted and curled like living things. The melody was no longer just a sound—it was a presence, filling the space with an oppressive weight that pressed down on him from all sides.

Eryx turned slowly, his sword raised in a defensive stance. The forest was no longer still; the trees seemed to sway in rhythm with the melody, their branches creaking and groaning as though alive. The threads began to appear, faint and shimmering, weaving through the air like ghostly veins.

At the edge of the clearing, a figure stepped forward.

It was Liora.

At least, it looked like her. She wore the same clothes, her hair falling in dark waves around her shoulders. But her eyes were different—brighter, almost glowing, and filled with an unsettling calm. Threads coiled around her wrists, their faint light pulsing in time with the melody.

"Liora?" Eryx called, his voice cracking.

She didn't respond immediately, her gaze fixed on him with an intensity that made his skin crawl. When she finally spoke, her voice was soft, almost melodic, blending seamlessly with the Caravan's song.

"Why did you stop me, Eryx?" she asked, her tone devoid of anger but heavy with something else—disappointment, perhaps, or sadness.

"I didn't stop you," he said, his grip tightening on his sword. "I tried to save you."

"Save me?" she repeated, tilting her head. "From what?"

"From this," he said, gesturing to the threads that bound her. "From them."

Liora stepped closer, the threads trailing behind her like a shimmering veil. "You don't understand," she said. "The Caravan isn't what you think it is. It's not just a curse. It's a story. A dance. And now, it's mine to lead."

Eryx's stomach twisted. "What are you talking about?" he demanded. "The Caravan is a prison. It takes people and turns them into puppets. It's not something you can control."

"But I can," she said, her voice steady. "Because I'm not fighting it anymore. I've seen what it truly is. The Caravan isn't just about taking—it's about weaving. It's about connection."

"You sound like them," Eryx said, his voice hardening. "This isn't you, Liora."

She smiled faintly, the expression both familiar and alien. "Maybe it's always been me," she said. "Maybe this is who I was meant to be."

The threads around her began to move, stretching toward Eryx like fingers reaching for him. He stepped back, his sword flashing in the dim light as he slashed at them. The threads recoiled, but only slightly, their movements slow and deliberate.

"Don't fight it," Liora said, her voice softening. "It's not trying to hurt you."

"Then what is it trying to do?" he asked, his voice trembling despite himself.

"It's offering you a choice," she said. "To join the dance. To be part of something greater."

Eryx shook his head, his chest tightening. "I've seen what happens to people who join," he said. "They lose themselves. They become shadows."

"They only lose themselves if they resist," Liora said. "But if you embrace it, you don't lose anything. You gain everything."

Her words sent a chill down his spine. He had heard similar promises before—from the Caravan's hunters, from the voices in the Maze, from the whispers in the threads. But hearing them from Liora made them cut deeper, striking at the core of his doubt.

"What if you're wrong?" he asked, his voice barely audible. "What if this is just another way for the Caravan to take everything from you?"

She hesitated, her glowing eyes dimming slightly. For a moment, she looked like the Liora he had known—the fierce, determined woman who had fought alongside him through the Maze, who had defied the Caravan at every turn. But the moment passed, and the glow returned, stronger than before.

"I'm not wrong," she said. "The Caravan showed me the truth. And I want to show it to you."

The threads moved again, faster this time, wrapping around Eryx's wrists before he could react. He tensed, expecting the same suffocating pull he had felt years ago when the Caravan had first marked him. But instead, the threads were warm, almost comforting, their touch light and gentle.

"Let go, Eryx," Liora said, stepping closer. "Let it in."

He closed his eyes, his mind racing. Every instinct screamed at him to fight, to cut the threads and run. But another part of him—the part that had always wondered if resistance was futile—hesitated.

"I can't," he said, his voice breaking. "I can't lose myself again."

"You won't," she said, her voice barely above a whisper. "I promise."

He opened his eyes, meeting her gaze. The threads tightened around his wrists, their warmth spreading through him like fire. The melody grew louder, drowning out his thoughts, until all he could hear was the song.

And then, everything went still.

The clearing vanished, replaced by a vast, endless void filled with light and shadow. The threads surrounded him, weaving through the air in intricate patterns that seemed to tell a story he couldn't quite understand. Liora was there, her presence a constant, guiding force that anchored him.

"This is the dance," she said, her voice echoing in the void. "It's not about control. It's about harmony. About letting go of fear."

He looked at her, his chest tightening. "And if I can't let go?"

"Then the dance will go on without you," she said. "But you'll always feel its pull."

Eryx closed his eyes, the warmth of the threads enveloping him. For the first time in years, the weight of his fear and guilt began to lift. The melody swelled, its rhythm syncing with his heartbeat, and he felt a strange, unshakable peace.

The Last Dance

When he opened his eyes, the void was gone. The clearing was silent, the threads faded, and Liora stood before him, her glow dimmed but steady.

"You chose the dance," she said, a faint smile on her lips.

Eryx nodded, his grip on his sword loosening. "I chose you."

The Caravan's melody lingered in the air, a quiet reminder that the story was far from over. But for the first time, Eryx felt ready to face it—not as a prisoner, but as a part of something greater. The dance would continue, and so would he.

Twenty-One

Love Beyond Time

The forest was bathed in a strange, ethereal light, a pale glow that seemed to come from nowhere and everywhere all at once. The air felt heavy, laden with the weight of stories untold and destinies unfurled. The melody of the Caravan lingered faintly in the background, a haunting tune that resonated in the space between Liora and Eryx. They stood together at the edge of an unfamiliar clearing, their breaths mingling in the cool, damp air.

For a moment, it felt like time itself had paused.

Eryx glanced at Liora, his gaze lingering on the faint glow that still radiated from her. She looked like herself, yet different. The threads that once bound her were gone, replaced by a subtle shimmer that danced across her skin. Her eyes, brighter and more intense than ever, seemed to hold the weight of countless lifetimes.

"Are you still... you?" Eryx asked, his voice hesitant.

Liora turned to him, her expression soft but unreadable. "I don't know," she admitted. "I feel... connected. To the Caravan. To the threads. To everything. But I'm still me, Eryx. I promise."

He wanted to believe her, but the change in her was undeniable. She wasn't just Liora anymore; she was something more. Something other.

The silence between them stretched, broken only by the faint rustle of leaves in the breeze. Finally, Liora spoke, her voice quiet but firm. "We need to keep moving. The Caravan's story isn't finished."

Eryx hesitated, his chest tightening. "What happens when we find the end of the story?" he asked. "Do you leave with it?"

She didn't answer right away, her gaze fixed on the horizon. "I don't know," she said finally. "But if that's what it takes to stop this, to free the people it's taken, then yes."

The words hit him like a blow, but he swallowed his protest. He had known from the moment they stepped into the Maze that this journey would demand sacrifices. He just hadn't expected one of those sacrifices to be her.

As they stepped into the clearing, the light shifted, taking on a golden hue that warmed the air. The trees around them bent and twisted, their branches weaving together to form an archway. At its center stood a stone platform, its surface etched with intricate carvings that pulsed faintly with light.

"This is it," Liora said, her voice tinged with awe. "The final thread."

Eryx followed her gaze, his heart pounding. The platform radiated power, its glow intensifying with each step they took. As they approached, the melody of the Caravan grew louder, swelling into a symphony that seemed to fill the entire clearing.

"What do we do?" he asked, his voice barely audible over the music.

Liora stepped onto the platform, her movements slow and deliberate. The carvings beneath her feet flared to life, their light forming a web of intricate patterns that spread outward, connecting to the trees, the ground, and the very air around them.

"I have to weave the final thread," she said, her voice steady despite the weight of her words. "It's the only way to end this."

Eryx's stomach twisted. "What does that mean?" he demanded. "What happens when you weave it?"

She turned to him, her eyes glistening with unshed tears. "It means I become part of the Caravan," she said. "Forever."

"No," he said, shaking his head. "There has to be another way."

"There isn't," she said, her voice soft but firm. "The Caravan needs a weaver, Eryx. Without one, the threads will unravel, and everything it's connected to will fall apart."

"Then let it fall apart," he said, his voice rising. "Let it end."

"It's not that simple," she said. "The Caravan isn't just a curse. It's a balance. It weaves stories, connects lives. If it disappears, so does everything it's touched."

Her words hung in the air, heavy and unyielding. Eryx's mind raced, his heart pounding as he searched for an argument, a solution, anything that could change her mind. But deep down, he knew she was right.

"Liora," he said, his voice breaking. "There has to be another way."

She stepped toward him, her hands reaching for his. The warmth of her touch sent a shiver through him, grounding him in the moment. "Eryx," she said, her voice trembling. "I'm not afraid. Because I know you'll remember me. And as long as someone remembers, I won't be truly gone."

"I don't want to remember you," he said, his throat tightening. "I want you here. With me."

Tears slipped down her cheeks, but she smiled, a bittersweet expression that cut deeper than any blade. "You'll always have me," she said. "In every thread, in every story. I'll be there."

The platform beneath her feet began to pulse, the light spreading outward in rippling waves. The melody of the Caravan swelled, its haunting tune filling the air with a sense of finality.

"Eryx," she said, her voice soft but urgent. "You have to let me go."

He shook his head, his grip on her hands tightening. "I can't," he said, his voice barely audible.

"You can," she said. "You've always been stronger than you think."

The light around her grew brighter, enveloping her in a golden glow. The threads appeared, weaving through the air in intricate patterns that spiraled toward the platform. They wrapped around Liora, their touch gentle but firm, binding her to the Caravan's story.

"Liora!" Eryx shouted, his voice raw with desperation.

She looked at him one last time, her eyes filled with love and sorrow. "Thank you," she said. "For everything."

And then she was gone.

The light flared, blinding and all-consuming, before fading into silence. The threads vanished, the platform dimming until it was little more than a cold, lifeless stone. The melody of the Caravan lingered for a moment longer, a faint echo of its former self, before disappearing entirely.

Eryx fell to his knees, his chest heaving as he stared at the empty platform. The weight of the moment crushed him, the loss of her presence an ache that would never fully heal. But as he sat there, the wind stirred, carrying with it the faintest hint of her voice.

"You're not alone, Eryx. You never will be."

He closed his eyes, the memory of her smile etched into his mind. And as the forest fell silent around him, he vowed to honor her sacrifice—to carry her story forward, to ensure she was never forgotten.

Love, he realized, wasn't bound by time or space. It existed beyond the threads, beyond the Caravan, beyond everything. It was eternal.

Just like her.

Twenty-Two

The Eternal Caravan Restored

The Eternal Caravan Restored

The clearing was quiet, unnaturally so. Eryx sat on the edge of the cold stone platform, his sword laid across his lap and his head bowed in exhaustion. The air was heavy with the absence of sound, a stark contrast to the symphony that had filled it moments ago. The golden light of the Caravan had faded, replaced by a gray, colorless dawn that bled through the treetops. Liora was gone, and with her, the threads that had bound the Caravan to its eternal cycle.

For the first time in what felt like years, Eryx was alone. But the forest did not remain silent for long. A faint hum began to stir in the distance, low and resonant, like the plucking of a single string on an ancient instrument. Eryx's head snapped up, his instincts sharpening. The sound grew louder, weaving its way through the trees with a haunting familiarity. It wasn't the melody of the Caravan, not exactly, but it carried echoes of it—notes of a song that was both new and impossibly old.

The ground beneath him began to pulse, faint tremors rippling through the earth like the echo of a heartbeat. Eryx scrambled to his feet, his hand instinctively going to his sword. The platform glowed faintly underfoot, the carvings on its surface reigniting with a soft, steady light.

"What is this?" he whispered, his voice hoarse.

The hum intensified, and with it came movement. Threads began to appear in the air, faint and shimmering, weaving through the clearing in slow, deliberate patterns. They weren't like the threads he remembered; these were softer, their glow warm and inviting. They moved with purpose, intertwining and looping in intricate designs that seemed almost playful.

Eryx backed away, his pulse quickening as the threads

converged on the platform. They spiraled upward, forming a column of light that shimmered and shifted like a living thing. The hum grew louder, resonating in his chest, until the column burst outward, filling the clearing with a golden radiance.

From the light, a figure emerged.

Eryx's breath caught in his throat. It was Liora.

She stood at the center of the platform, her hair cascading around her shoulders like a dark river, her eyes glowing with a soft, golden light. The threads coiled around her wrists and ankles, but they didn't bind her—they moved with her, as if responding to her will. She looked both radiant and untouchable, a being of light and shadow who seemed to exist beyond the confines of the mortal world.

"Liora?" Eryx said, his voice trembling.

She turned to him, her gaze locking onto his. There was a moment of silence, and then she smiled—a small, familiar smile that made his chest ache with equal parts relief and sorrow.

"I'm here," she said, her voice soft but resonant.

Eryx took a cautious step forward, his hands trembling. "You... you're back?"

"In a way," she said, her expression bittersweet. "I'm part of the Caravan now, Eryx. But it's different. The story is different."

"What does that mean?" he asked, his voice thick with emotion.

Liora stepped off the platform, the threads trailing behind her like a cloak. "The Caravan was never meant to be a curse," she said. "It was created to connect people, to weave their stories together. But over time, it became corrupted. The threads were twisted into something dark, something that took instead of gave."

"And now?" Eryx asked, his throat tightening.

"Now, it's restored," she said. "The threads are whole again. They won't bind or trap—they'll guide and protect."

Eryx wanted to believe her, but the memory of what the Caravan had done was too fresh, too raw. "How do you know it won't turn dark again?" he asked, his voice low.

"Because I'm its weaver now," Liora said, her tone firm. "I won't let it happen."

The certainty in her voice sent a wave of conflicting emotions through him. He was relieved that she was alive—sort of. Grateful that the Caravan's curse had been broken. But the realization that she was no longer fully his Liora, that she belonged to something greater now, was a bitter pill to swallow.

"So, what happens now?" he asked, his voice barely audible.

Liora stepped closer, the threads around her shifting and shimmering like liquid light. "Now, the Caravan begins again," she said. "But this time, it will be different. It will bring people together instead of tearing them apart."

Eryx searched her eyes, looking for the woman he had fought beside, the woman he had come to care for more than he cared to admit. She was still there, but she was more than that now. She was something bigger, something beyond him.

"And what about us?" he asked, the words slipping out before he could stop them.

Liora's expression softened, and she reached out, her fingers brushing against his. The warmth of her touch sent a shiver through him, grounding him in the moment. "We'll always have a part in the story," she said. "But my path is different now."

Eryx swallowed hard, his chest tightening. "I don't want to lose you," he said, his voice breaking.

"You won't," she said, her voice a whisper. "I'll always be here, in the threads, in the stories they weave. And you'll always be a part of me."

The hum of the Caravan grew louder, the threads around her glowing brighter. The light of the platform flared, and the clearing seemed to shift, the trees bending and warping as if responding to the Caravan's presence. Eryx felt the ground tremble beneath his feet, the air thick with energy.

"Eryx," Liora said, her voice cutting through the chaos. "You have to let me go."

He shook his head, his eyes stinging with unshed tears. "I can't," he said. "Not again."

"You can," she said, her tone steady but kind. "You're stronger than you know. And the Caravan isn't the end of our story—it's just the beginning."

The light around her intensified, the threads weaving into a brilliant tapestry that filled the clearing. Eryx shielded his eyes, his heart pounding as the melody of the Caravan swelled into a crescendo. When the light finally dimmed, she was gone.

The clearing was still, the air heavy with silence. The platform remained, its carvings faintly glowing, but the threads had vanished. The melody of the Caravan was a faint echo, barely audible, as if it were retreating into the distance.

Eryx stood alone, his sword at his side, his chest tight with grief and resolve. He turned his gaze to the sky, where the first rays of dawn were breaking through the trees.

The Caravan was restored, its curse lifted, its purpose renewed. And though Liora was gone, her presence lingered in the threads, in the light, in the stories yet to be told.

And as Eryx took his first step out of the clearing, he knew that their story was far from over. It would live on, not just in the threads of the Caravan, but in the hearts of those who carried it forward.

In him.

www.ingramcontent.com/pod-product-compliance
Lightning Source LLC
LaVergne TN
LVHW011945070526
838202LV00054B/4808